THE ERA

OF THE

PROTESTANT REVOLUTION

BY

FREDERIC SEEBOHM

AUTHOR OF

' THE OXFORD REFORMERS—COLET, ERASMUS, AND MORE'

SECOND EDITION

With Notes on Books in English relating to the Reformation,
by GEO. P. FISHER, D.D., Professor of Ecclesiastical
History in Yale College, author of " *History
of the Reformation*," &c.

AMS PRESS
NEW YORK

Reprinted from the edition of 1903, New York

First AMS EDITION published 1971

Manufactured in the United States of America

International Standard Book Number: 0-404-05695-4

Library of Congress Catalog Number: 77-147114

AMS PRESS INC.
NEW YORK, N.Y.   10003

SUMMARY.

PART I.

STATE OF CHRISTENDOM.

CHAPTER I.

INTRODUCTORY.

CHAPTER II.

THE POWERS BELONGING TO THE OLD ORDER OF THINGS,
AND GOING OUT.

CHAPTER III.

THE MODERN NATIONS WHICH WERE RISING INTO POWER.

CHAPTER IV.

THE NEED OF REFORM AND DANGER OF REVOLUTION.

PART II.

THE PROTESTANT REVOLUTION.

CHAPTER I.

REVIVAL OF LEARNING AND REFORM AT FLORENCE.

CHAPTER II.

THE OXFORD REFORMERS.

CHAPTER III.

THE WITTENBERG REFORMERS.

CHAPTER IV.

THE CRISIS.—REFORM OR REVOLUTION.—REFORM REFUSED
BY THE RULING POWERS.

PART III.

RESULTS OF THE PROTESTANT REVOLUTION.

CHAPTER I.

REVOLTS FROM ROME.

(1.) IN SWITZERLAND AND GERMANY.

CHAPTER II.

REVOLT OF ENGLAND FROM ROME.,

CHAPTER VIII.

ECONOMIC RESULTS OF THE ERA.

CONCLUSION.

ERA

OF THE

PROTESTANT REVOLUTION.

PART I.

STATE OF CHRISTENDOM.

CHAPTER I.

INTRODUCTORY.

(a) The Small Extent of Christendom.

IN the map at the beginning of this volume the light
portion marks the Old World as it was known at the
commencement of the era of which we have to speak.

A glance will show how small a portion of the known
world belonged to Christendom—that marked *red* and
striped red. And only the *red* part belonged
to Western or Roman Christendom, with
which we have mostly to do. The part *striped*
red had long ago severed itself from the Western and
belonged to the Eastern Church, which by the Roman
was regarded as heretical and alien. Thus the Christendom of which Rome was the capital embraced only
the western half of the little peninsula of Europe. And
not even *all* that. For there was a little bit of Spain
(marked blue) which did not belong to Christendom.

The smallness of Christendom.

B

We may note next how much smaller Christendom was than it had once been. It had once covered not only

Smaller than it once had been.

the parts coloured red and striped red, but also those coloured dark blue, *i. e.* all Europe, Asia Minor, and the African shores of the Mediterranean Sea. But the dark blue portions had been conquered from Christendom by her great rival Moham-

The Mohammedan power.

medan power, whose religion, though only half as old as Christianity, was thought to number many times as many adherents as there were Christians, and covered a much larger area than Christendom—all the countries marked *blue*.

More than 700 years—twenty generations—ago the Mohammedan Moors, after conquering the African shores

Checked in the West.

of the Mediterranean, had pushed on into Spain and threatened Christendom from the West. Defeated and checked at the great battle of Tours in 732, after a struggle of 700 years they still held a foot-hold in Spain—the rich southern province of Granada.

But whilst checked in the West, Mohammedan arms had recently been encroaching more and more upon

But encroaching from the East.

Christendom from the East. Turkey and Hungary had fallen into their hands, and in 1453, *i. e.* in the lifetime of the fathers of the men of the new era, Constantinople had been taken by the Turks. The old capital of the Eastern Roman Empire now became the capital of the great Ottoman Empire. We see then how near to Rome Turkish conquests had come. Only the Adriatic separated the Ottoman Empire from Italy. Once the Turks had even got a footing in the heel of Italy. It really seemed not unlikely that the capital of Christendom might itself some day fall into their hands.

No wonder the Turks were the terror of the Christians. And yet they had one thing in common, and it is well that we should remember it. They were worshippers of the same God. Both Christians and Mohammedans professed to trace back their faith to Abraham. Though Christendom was small and dwindling, the area of the religion inherited from Abraham was large and increasing. But this was no consolation to men to whom their fellow Christians of the Eastern Church were heretics, the 'unbelieving Jews' the objects of scorn, and the 'infidel' Turks of terror.

Kinship between Christians, Mohammedans, and Jews.

But they hate one another.

(b) *The Signs of New Life in Christendom.*

Christendom had never felt herself so small or so beset with enemies. And yet there were signs of a new life springing up. The new era was to be one of hope and progress.

The Crusades of the Christian nations, intended to dislodge the 'Infidel' out of Jerusalem, though they had failed in that object, had awakened Europe to new life. East and West were brought nearer together. Knights and soldiers and pilgrims brought home from new lands new thoughts and wider notions. Commerce with the East was extended. Maritime enterprise was stimulated. There was improvement in ships. The mariner's compass was discovered, and under its guidance longer voyages could safely be made. The invention of gunpowder had changed the character of war and enlarged the scale on which it was waged. The recent conquests of the Turks were indirectly the cause of new life to Christendom. The fall of Constantinople resulted in a great revival of

Influence of the Crusades.

Inventions.

Fall of Constantinople.

Revival of learning.

learning in Europe. Driven from the East, learned Greeks and Jews came to settle in Italy. Greek and Hebrew were again studied in Europe. The literature, the history, the poetry, the philosophy and arts of old Greece and Rome were revived. And the result was that a succession of poets, painters, sculptors, and historians sprang up in Christendom such as had not been

Printing. known for centuries. Above all the invention of printing had come just in time to spread whatever new ideas were afloat with a rapidity never known before.

(c) *The Widening of Christendom.*

So it is easy to see there were abundant signs of new life in Christendom, however small, and hemmed in, and threatened she might be. A new era was coming on, and now observe how Christendom was widened, and fresh room found for the civilization of the new era to work in.

(1) In 1491 the Moors were at last and for ever driven

Moors driven out of Spain. out of Spain by the conquest of Granada by Ferdinand and Isabella, and men felt that a turn had come in the tide of victory in favour of Christians.

(2) In 1492 came the discovery of the New World by Columbus, followed up by the Spanish conquests of

Discovery of America. Mexico and Peru, the Portuguese settlements in Brazil, and the gaining of a foothold in the New World by Sebastian Cabot for England —the embryo of those great colonies, the New England, or extension of England across the Atlantic, in which half the English people now dwell.

(3) In 1497 Vasco de Gama sailed for the first time round the Cape of Good Hope, and a new way was

opened to Asia and the East Indies, and New way to East Indies.
out of this in the far future came England's
Indian Empire and Australian colonies.

Looking again at the map, and adding to the Old
World the countries coloured in shadow which were
brought to light mostly during the childhood of the men
of the new era, we cannot wonder that they spoke of
them as belonging to a '*new* world.' And bearing in
mind that having reached the West Indies, knowing of
no Pacific Ocean between, they thought they had
reached the East Indies from the west, and so had been,
as it were, *round the world*, we may realize how grand
the new discoveries must have seemed to them. Men of
that day did not of course realize what we know now,
how wide a field these new discoveries would open for
Christian civilization to extend itself into. But still they
gave an immediate feeling of relief to pent-up Christen-
dom, a spur to commerce and maritime en- Men's minds prepared for great events.
terprise, new light to science, new sources
of wealth, and new direction to the energies
of nations, and more or less to all men a sense that they
were living in an age of progress and change which prepared them to look into the future with hope, and to expect great events to happen in their time.

(*d*) *The New Era one of Progress in Civilization.
In what Modern Civilization Consists.*

The work of the new era was to gain for Christendom
a fresh step in the onward course of civilization.

And when we speak of advance in *civilization*, what
do we mean ? Not simply advance in popu- What civiliza-tion is.
lation, wealth, luxury, but far more, that
which is hid in the derivation of the word,
viz., *advance in the art of living together in civil society.*

And in order clearly to understand the work that was to be done in this era of progress, we must understand the difference between (1) the old form of civilization which was to be left behind and (2) the new form of civilization towards which fresh steps were to be gained.

(1) The old Roman civilization had come about by the conquest of the uncivilized tribes of Western Europe

The old Roman civilization. by the Romans, by their making the known world into one great empire, bringing all its ends together by making roads, encouraging commerce, making the Latin language understood by the educated all over it, and Rome the centre of it all. The Roman Empire was in fact a network of Roman towns, with all the threads of it drawn towards Rome. These towns were camps, from which the conquerors ruled the districts round. Little account was taken of the country people.

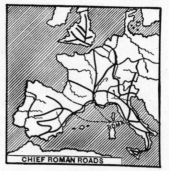

CHIEF ROMAN ROADS

They were looked upon as hopelessly rustic and barbarian. Under this system all the conquered countries were made provinces of the Roman Empire, not for their

Its main vice. own but for the conquerors' good. The masses of the people were governed by Roman governors for the benefit, not of themselves, but of a small number of Roman citizens. This vice—this blot —in the Roman polity was no doubt the cause of its decay.

(2) The aim of modern civilization is obviously far
higher than this. It has not yet reached its   Modern
goal, but we see clearly that it has been   civilization.
aiming, not at one vast universal empire,
but at the formation of several compact and separate
nations, living peaceably side by side, respecting one
another's rights and freedom; and, looking within each
nation, at making all classes of the people, town and
country, rich and poor, alike citizens for whose common
weal the nation is to be governed, and who   Its strength.
ultimately shall govern themselves. In this
aim of modern civilization *to secure the common weal of
the people* lies its power and strength.

Now the passage from the old decaying form of civilization to the new, better, and stronger one, involved a
change; and this change must needs take   The crisis of
place slowly and by degrees. The old order   the struggle
of things had gradually for long been going   old and the
out: the new order of things had gradually   new order of
for long been coming in. But in this era   things.
was to be the *crisis* of the change—the final decisive
struggle between the two forces; and in this lies its
importance and its interest.

Before we begin the story of this struggle, we must
briefly consider what it was in the state of   Plan of this
Christendom which brought it on; and this   book.
will be done best by our examining—

(1) The powers which belonged to the old order of
things, and now dying out.

(2) The state of the modern nations which were
growing up in their place.

In doing so, we shall try to lay most stress on the
condition of the masses of the people; and we shall not
fail to see clearly some of the main points in which, if

modern civilization was to go on, there was a necessity for reform, and the danger there was that, if the needful reforms were much longer withheld, there would be revolution.

Then in Part II. will come the story of the struggle; and in Part III. its results on the different nations. We shall end with trying to take stock of the amount of progress gained during the era, and to look forward at the prospects of the future that arise out of it.

CHAPTER II.

THE POWERS BELONGING TO THE OLD ORDER OF THINGS, AND GOING OUT.

(a) *The Ecclesiastical System.*

WESTERN CHRISTENDOM was united under one Ecclesiastical system—the Roman, or, as it called itself, the 'Holy Catholic' Church.

It was, in fact, a great Ecclesiastical Empire, of which Rome was the capital, and the Pope of Rome the head.

The Ecclesiastical Empire, and Rome the capital.

In the last generation there had been a schism—*i. e.* for a while there were two rival Popes excommunicating each other—but after much trouble and scandal the schism had been ended, and now all was one again.

Europe was mapped out into ecclesiastical provinces, at the head of each of which was an archbishop. Each province was divided into dioceses, with bishops at their head, and each diocese into parishes, each with its parish priest. Thus there was an ecclesiastical network all over Europe, all the threads of which were drawn towards

Rome, and held in the hands of the Pope and his cardinals.

This ecclesiastical empire kept itself as free as possible from the civil power in each nation. It considered itself above kings and princes. It was more ancient than any of their thrones and kingdoms. Kings were not secure on their thrones till they had the sanction of the Church. On the other hand the clergy claimed to be free from prosecution under the criminal laws of the lands they lived in. They struggled to keep their own ecclesiastical laws and their own ecclesiastical courts, receiving authority direct from Rome, and with final appeal, not to the Crown, but to the Pope.

Independent of the civil power.

In addition to the parochial clergy, there were orders of monks. The two chief of them were the rival orders of the Dominican and Augustinian monks; and in most towns there were one, two, or half-a-dozen monasteries and cloisters. So numerous were the monks that they swarmed everywhere, and had become, by the favour of the Popes, more important and powerful in many ways than the parochial clergy.

The monks.

It is essential to mark what a power this ecclesiastical empire wielded over the nations. The ecclesiastics held in their hands the keys, as it were, not only of heaven but of earth.

Power of the ecclesiastical system,

They alone baptized; they alone married people (though unmarried themselves); they alone could grant a divorce. They had the charge of men on their death-beds; they alone buried, and could refuse Christian burial in the churchyards. They alone had the disposition of the goods of deceased persons. When a man made a will, it had to be proved in their ecclesiastical courts. If men disputed

by influence over the people;

their claims, doubted their teaching, or rebelled from their doctrines, they virtually condemned them to the stake, by handing them over to the civil power, which acted in submission to their dictates. You will see at once how great a power all these things must have given them over the minds, the fears, the happiness, and the lives of the people.

The ordinary revenues of the clergy were large. They *by its wealth;* had a right to ' tithes;' *i. e.* to a tenth part of the produce of the whole land of Christendom. This had belonged to them for hundreds of years. In addition to this they claimed fees for everything they did.

The monks, according to the rules of their founders, ought to have got their living by begging alms in return for their preachings and their prayers for the living and the dead. But their vow of poverty had not kept them poor. People thought that by giving property to them they could save their souls; so rich men, sometimes in their lifetime but oftener on their deathbeds, left them large sums of money and estates in land. In spite of laws passed by the civil powers to prevent it, it was said that they had got about a third of the land of Europe into their possession. Thus the revenue and riches of the Church was far larger than that of the kings and princes of Europe.

These were not the sole secrets of their power. From the fact that the clergy were almost the only educated *by the mono-* people in Europe, they became the lawyers *poly of learn-* and diplomatists, envoys, ambassadors, min- *ing,* isters, chancellors, and even prime ministers of princes. They were mixed up with the politics of Europe, and the reins of the State in most countries **were** in the hands of ecclesiastics. They received pro·

motion to bishoprics most often in return for and political such political services.   influence,

We cannot fail to see how vast the political power of such an ecclesiastical empire as this must have been. The Pope, through his army of ecclesiastics all over Christendom, had the strings in his hand by which to influence the politics of Europe. And one which all cen- of the great complaints of the best men of tred in Rome. the day was that this political influence was used by Rome for her own ends instead of the good of Europe, and that the immense ecclesiastical revenues tended to flow out of the provinces into the coffers of the Popes and cardinals of Rome.

WHITE REVOLTED FROM ROME.

All this of course tended to hinder the This Empire growth and in- will be dependence of broken up. the separate nations, and to prevent all classes within them from becoming united into a compact nation.

It will be one great work of the era, to break up this ecclesiastical empire—to free several nations (those mark- ed white on the map) from its yoke. So that Rome will cease to be the capital of Christendom.

(b) *The Scholastic System.*

There was another power in Europe which was Roman and not national; which tended to keep classes of people apart, and so stood in the way of the growth of national life in the separate nations.

The learned world was a world of its own, severed

from the masses of the people by its scholastic system.

The learned world talked and wrote Latin, All the learned men in Europe talked and wrote letters and books in Latin—the language of Rome. Some of them did not 'even know the common language of the countries they lived in. And as Latin was the language of learning, so Rome was the capital of the learned world. Thus the learned world was closely connected with the ecclesiastical system. Learned people were looked upon as belonging to the clergy; and the Pope had long *and belonged to the clergy.* claimed them as subjects of his ecclesiastical empire. So for centuries in England a man convicted of a crime, by pleading that he could read and write, could claim benefit of clergy, *i. e.* to be tried in an ecclesiastical court, and this by long abuse came to mean exemption from the punishments of the criminal law of the land.

This tended to give to knowledge and learning itself a clerical or scholastic character. Knowledge was tied *This made learning 'scholastic,'* down by scholastic rules which had grown up in times when the ecclesiastics were the only educated people. The old learned men— 'the schoolmen' as they were called—looked at everything with ecclesiastical eyes. All knowledge had thus got to be looked upon almost as a part of theology. Matters of science—*e. g.* whether the earth moved round *shackled science,* the sun or the sun round the earth—were settled by texts from the Bible, instead of by examining into the facts. So there was no freedom of inquiry even in scientific matters. A man who made discoveries in science might be stopped and punished if he found out that the old schoolmen were wrong in anything.

Under the scholastic system the Christian religion,

which in the days of Christ and the apostles was a thing of the heart (love of God and one's neighbour), and religion had grown into a theology—a thing of the also, head. The chief handybook of the theology of the schoolmen was a great folio volume of more than 1,000 pages.

Thus the scholastic system necessarily kept both science and religion the property of a clerical class, and out of the hands of the common people, to whom Latin was a dead language; while at the and kept same time it kept the learning even of the them from the common learned world shackled by scholastic rules. people.

It is important to see this clearly, because one great part of the work of the new era was to throw the gates of knowledge open to all men, and to set Necessity of the minds of men free from this clerical or mental freedom. scholastic thraldom—to· set both science and religion free, for freedom was as important to the one as it was to the other. Without it there could be no real progress in civilization.

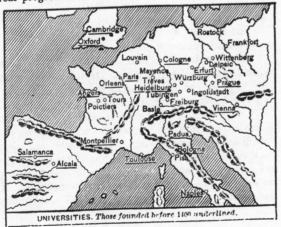

UNIVERSITIES. *Those founded before 1400 underlined.*

The Universi-
ties. The universities were the great centres of the learned world.

There were thirty or forty of them scattered over Europe, and they were in more or less close connexion with each other. They are marked on the map, and the chief of them should be carefully remembered. The oldest and most celebrated were *Oxford* and *Cambridge* in England, *Paris* and *Orleans* in France, *Bologna* and *Padua* in Italy, and *Salamanca* in Spain, *Prague* in Bohemia, and *Cologne* in Germany. These, at the beginning of the era of the Reformation, were all more than a hundred, and some two hundred years old. The youngest university in Europe was that of *Wittenberg*, founded in 1502 by the Elector of Saxony.

Students were in the habit of passing from one university to another. Oxford students would pass on to Paris, and from Paris to Bologna, to take their degrees. And wherever there happened to be a famous professor, thither students from all other universities flocked.

Students pass
from one to
another.

Now the result of this was very important.

As one example, we may take the great movement in the fourteenth century in the direction of reform.

Wiclif wrote books in Latin at Oxford. They were copied and read all over Europe. Oxford students went to the newly-opened university at Prague. Wiclif's writings made as much noise, and were as well known in Bohemia as they were in England. Huss and Jerome of Prague became the Bohemian successors of the English Wiclif, and thus the movement in favour of reform was transplanted from one country to another. What was discussed among the learned soon trickled down into the common talk of the people. So there arose out of Wiclif's movement

The result of
this in the days
of Wiclif.

the Lollard insurrection in England and the Hussite wars in Bohemia.

What had thus happened before in the days when books were multiplied only by the slow work of the pen was still more likely to happen again in the days of the printing press.

We shall see how in the new era these things were repeated—how the spirit of revival of learning and religious reform spread, first among the learned from university to university by students passing from one to another, now in Italy, now into *Will be repeated in the new era.* England, now into Germany, and how at last it trickled down into the minds of the common people all over Europe.

The fact that both the ecclesiastical system and the learned world were coextensive with Christendom, and so closely united together, gave to Christendom a unity which alone made the work of the era possible. It was as though, in spite of distance and the difficulties of travelling, learned men were nearer together than even now, in these *The work of the era.* days of railroads and steamboats and telegraphs. The work of the era was to rend Christendom asunder. Rome was no longer to be her capital. The Pope was no longer to be recognized everywhere as her spiritual head. The Latin language was no longer to be the common tongue of literature and books all over Europe. Young nations were to divide Europe between them, to have their own churches and clergy, their own languages, their own literature, their own learned men and universities, and so to become more independent of each other and of Rome. And this was one of the stages through which Christian civilization was to pass in its onward course.

(*c*) *The Feudal System and the forces which were breaking it up.*

There was another system which was opposed to the

The feudal system. growth of modern nations—the feudal system. It belonged to the old order of things, and was fast decaying and going out.

Divided countries into petty lordships. The feudal system hindered the growth of free nations, not by tending too much to keep up the unity of Christendom, but by dividing countries up into innumerable petty lordships.

Each feudal lord was a little sovereign both as regards those below him—his vassals and serfs—and also as regards his fellows, except so far as he and they were controlled by higher feudal powers above them. He waged what petty wars he chose with his neighbours, and lorded it over his vassals and serfs, whilst himself very jealously resisting any unusual interference from powers above him.

Decay of the feudal system. The feudal system had already shown signs of falling to pieces, and in some countries had very much died out.

In some countries the petty lordships had fallen quite under the power of the Crown.

By a long process, some of the feudal lords had grown

Subjection of feudal lords to the Crown. in power, while the multitude of smaller ones had sunk into ever-increasing insignificance. Especially in countries where by the rule of inheritance lordships descended only to the eldest male heir, there was a natural tendency for lordships to unite by marriage and inheritance. The greater families intermarried and grew richer, and the royal family was in fact the one which had grown so much bigger than the rest that it kept swallowing up more and more into itself. We shall see that it was so notably in France. The process went on more slowly in Germany, where the rule of inheritance was division among the male heirs, and so the tendency was towards more and more division, and an ever-increasing host of petty lordships. In Germany the feudal system was still in full force, and we shall see by-and-by how it prevented her from growing into a compact nation, and how much she had to suffer for want of the nobles being subjected to a central authority able to preserve the public peace and to curb their lawlessness and tyranny. But speaking generally, things were more and *Increasing power of the crown.* more working in the new era towards the complete subjection of the feudal nobility in each nation to the central power, *i. e.* towards the supremacy of the Crown.

But *commerce* was breaking up the feudal system faster than anything else, and commerce had its chief seat in the towns. Trade, commerce, and manufactures were the life of the towns. The little towns were the markets of the country round, and their trade lay between the peasantry and the bigger towns. *The growth of commerce.* These, in their turn, lived upon the share they had in that wider commerce of the world, of which, by the aid of Map No. 2 (at the beginning of this volume), we must now try to grasp the main features.

The Crusades had done much to open up a commerce between Asia and Europe. This commerce with the East was mostly in the hands of the *Trade of the Mediterranean.* great cities on the Mediterranean Sea. The new way to the Indies was not yet open. The products of the East, its spices and its silks, were carried overland from the Persian Gulf and Red Sea to the Levant, and then shipped to the ports of Italy. Silk manufactures were also carried on in Italy, in Catalonia in Spain, and at Lyons in France. These eastern products and silks were the chief exports of the Mediterranean merchants.

The commerce of the North Sea was equally important. The woollen manufactures of the north were its chief feature. Spain exported wool and some parts of Germany, but England was the great wool-growing country. The wool was woven into cloth in the looms of the eastern

The manu-
facturing
districts.

counties of England, and Flanders on the opposite shore of the North Sea. These were the chief manufacturing districts, though other towns in England, up the Rhine, and in Germany, had their weavers also. There were also considerable linen manufactures in the north of France.

The North Sea was the great fishing ground, and

The
fisheries.

dried fish was a great article of commerce when during Lent and on every Friday all Christendom lived upon fish.

There was also a trade in furs and skins with North Russia, Norway, and Sweden.

This commerce of the North was carried on by the Hanse towns—reaching from the shores of the Baltic

The com-
merce of the
Hanse towns.

westward to the Netherlands, and inland in Germany as far south as Cologne. There were eighty towns belonging to this league, and they had stations or factories at Novgorod, Bergen, London, and Bruges.

Bruges in Flanders had been, and now Antwerp was the great central mart of the commerce of the world.

Bruges and
Antwerp the
central marts
of commerce.

Here the merchants of the North exchanged their goods with the merchants of the Mediterranean. Here their ships met and divided the maritime commerce of the world between them. Here, too, the maritime met the inland and overland trade—inland trade with the German towns, overland trade down the Rhine, Lines of through Germany, over the Alps, by the maritime, Brenner and Julier passes into Italy. There inland, and overland was much trade between German and trade. Venetian merchants, and the contemporary historian, Machiavelli, states that all Italy was in a manner supplied with the commodities and manufactures of Germany. Since the Netherlands and Austria fell into the hands of the House of Hapsburg, and Maximilian was Emperor of Germany, there had also naturally sprung up a trade between the Rhine and the Danube.

These were the great lines of trade, and in these lines lay the chief commercial towns, living on their share in the commerce of the world.

Under the feudal system the towns had once been mostly subject to feudal lords, but they had The towns early shown their independent spirit, and re- had mostly belled, or bargained for charters of freedom. got free. A free town was a little republic, organized for protection from foes without and for peaceful trade within. The members of each trade were banded together into guilds for mutual protection, and there was generally a sort of representative government—an upper and lower council of citizens, by whom the town was governed.

We can easily understand how likely the towns were to hate the feudal lords, whose petty wars dis- Why the turbed the public peace and made commerce towns hated hazardous. They had to fortify themselves feudalism against these petty wars, and their cavalcades of merchandize had to be protected by soldiers on the roads. So there had grown up out of commerce an anti-feudal power in Europe. In almost every country the and favored towns banded themselves together against the Crown. the feudal system, and when the power of the

Crown began to rise, the towns were the stepping-stones by which it rose to the top. Kings invited the towns to send burgesses to the national Diets or Parliaments, and they were a growing power in almost every State.

There was yet another most numerous and most important class affected by feudalism—the peasantry.

The feudal peasantry. The peasants, under the feudal system, were more or less reduced to a condition of vassalage or serfdom.

Let us understand what this was. The tribes who conquered Northern and Western Europe were a land-

Once more free than under the feudal system. folk—people living by the land. They settled in villages, and all the land belonging to each village belonged to the community, as it does now in Swiss valleys. The people were tenants only of their little allotments, with common rights over the unallotted pasture, woods, forests, and rivers: *i. e.* they had a common or joint use of them.

Now the feudal system had put the feudal lords in the place of the community. The peasantry became tenants of these lords, paying rents sometimes in money, but chiefly in services of labour on their lords' lands. The lords, moreover, claimed more and more of the unallotted portion of the common lands as their own. The serfs were not allowed to leave their land, because it would rob the lords of their services. So the lords held their peasantry completely in their power. This was feudal serfdom when in full force. In some countries it was still in force, in others it had almost disappeared.

In those countries where the lords were most subjected

Where the central power was weakest, feudal serfdom lingered longest. to the Crown, as in France and England, the serfs were likely to be best off and farthest advanced on the road to freedom. In those in which the feudal lords were least ·subdued, and the central power least formed, as in Germany, we should expect to find feudal serfdom lingering on. And it was so.

As the towns were the enemies of the feudal nobility, so they were the friends of the feudal peasantry. Commerce introduced everywhere money payments instead of barter. Payment of rent in services of labour was an old-fashioned kind of barter. Commerce, therefore, helped to introduce money rents and money wages, and where these were early introduced, as in France and England, the condition of the peasant was much improved. But more than this; labour was often wanted in the towns: the wages paid in the towns often tempted the peasant to desert his land and feudal lord, and to flee to a town. The towns favoured this immigration into them of runaway serfs, and there grew up in some countries a settled rule of law that after residence in a town a year and a day they could not be reclaimed.

The towns and commerce favoured freedom of the peasantry.

Thus we see clearly how the feudal system was breaking up under the influence of commerce and the combined power of the towns and the Crown.

The petty lordships were becoming united into the larger unit of the nation, but we see on the other hand what a danger there was of the nation becoming divided into hostile *classes*. How were classes so contrarient as the feudal lords, the townspeople, and the peasantry, to be blended in one national life? This was the great problem modern civilization had to solve, and some nations succeeded much better than others in solving it.

CHAPTER III.

THE MODERN NATIONS WHICH WERE RISING INTO POWER.

(a) *Italy.*

No country had made less progress towards becoming,
Not a united nation. a compact and united nation than Italy, the very country in which Rome, the capital of Christendom, exercised most influence.

The contemporary historian, *Machiavelli*, shows how
Rome, according to Machiavelli, the cause of her disunity. Rome was the cause of Italy's ruin and disunity.

He says: 'Some are of opinion that the welfare of Italy depends upon the Church of Rome. I shall set down two unanswerable reasons to the contrary :—

'(1) By the corrupt example of that court Italy has lost its religion and become heathenish and irreligious.

'(2) We owe to Rome also that we are become divided and factious, which must of necessity be our ruin, for no nation was ever happy or united unless under the rule of one commonwealth or prince, as France and Spain are at this time. And the reason is that the Pope, though he claims temporal as well as spiritual jurisdiction, is not strong enough to rule all Italy himself, and whenever he sees any danger he calls in some foreign potentate to help him against any other power growing strong enough to be formidable. Therefore it is that, instead of getting united under one rule, Italy is split up into several principalities, and so disunited that it falls easily a prey to the power not only of the barbarians, but of any one who cares to invade it. This misfortune we Italians owe only to the Church of Rome.'

That these words of Machiavelli were too strictly true, we shall judge from the facts.

We have seen what was the power of Rome. If ex-erted in favour of Christian civilization how many bless-ings might not the Church have earned! Rome a centre But it was notorious to every one living at of rottenness. the time that Rome used her power so ill, and that her own character and that of her Popes were so evil, that she had become both politically and spirit-ually the centre of wickedness and rottenness in Europe and especially in Italy.

And this was no new thing. Men had been complain-ing of it for generations. The greatest poets of Italy had long before immortalized the guilt of Dante on the Rome. Two centuries before, Dante had Popes. described the Popes of his day as men

> whose avarice
> O'ercasts the world with mourning, under foot
> Treading the good, and raising bad men up.
> Of Shepherds like to you, the Evangelist
> Was ware, when her who sits upon the waves
> With kings in filthy whoredom he beheld!

And soon after Dante, Petrarch had de- Petrarch on scribed Rome thus :— Rome.

> Once Rome! now false and guilty Babylon!
> Hive of deceits! Terrible prison,
> Where the good doth die, the bad is fed and fattened!
> Hell of the living! . . . .
> Sad world that dost endure it! Cast her out!

And in the days of these great poets, men, Reformers and Councils too, had tried to reform Rome, but without avail. A few more generations had passed and Rome was now not only unreformed but in respect to morals worse than ever. How much worse we know not only from the censures of her poets, but from the facts of her contemporary historians.

The Popes of Rome had for long not only wielded both political and spiritual power, but used them to enrich their own families; and as a rule they had recently been notoriously bad men.

Recent Popes bad men.

Alexander VI. was the reigning Pope, and the worst Rome ever had. His wicked reign lasted from 1492 to 1503. His great aim was to bring Rome, and if he could, all Italy, into the hands of his still wickeder son Cæsar Borgia. The latter caused his own brother to be stabbed and thrown into the Tiber. He had his brother-in-law assassinated on his palace-steps. He stabbed one of his father's favourites who had taken shelter under the pontifical robes, so that the blood spirted into the Pope's face. Rich men were poisoned to get their wealth. The reign of these Borgias was a reign of terror in Rome. At last, in 1503, the Pope fell, it is said, into his own trap, and died of the poison he had prepared for another.

Alexander VI. and Cæsar Borgia.

Their crimes.

Another great Italian historian of the time, *Guicciardini*, records that the body of the Pope, black and loathsome, was exposed to public view in St. Peter's. And he goes on to say:—

"All Rome flocked to that sight, and could not sufficiently satiate their eyes with gazing on the remains of the extinct serpent, who by his immoderate ambition, pestiferous perfidy, monstrous lust, and every sort of horrible cruelty and unexampled avarice—selling without distinction property sacred and profane—had compassed the destruction of so many by poison, and was now become its victim!'

Machiavelli was right then, that the example of Rome in Italy was an evil one. That it made the Italians hate the Church, and drove thinking men, while they remained superstitious, to doubt Christianity, and to welcome even Pagan religions, because they seemed so much purer than that which Rome offered them, we shall see by-and-by. This is what he meant when he spoke of the Italians becoming 'heathenish'—it was exactly the fact.

Effects of the Pope's wickedness.

And now as to this other statement, that Rome was the cause of the divisions, and therefore of the ruin of Italy; this also, the facts of the recent history of Italy will make clear.

The map shows how Italy was in the main divided—Venice, Milan, and Florence to the north; Naples to the south; the States of the Church between.

Main divisions of Italy.

(1) *The States of the Church.* Over these the Popes had a shadowy kind of rule, but they were made up of petty lordships and cities, claiming independence, and even Rome was ruled by its Barons rather than by the Popes; or to speak more correctly the Barons and the Pope were always quarrelling which of the two should rule. The Pope lived in his strong castle of St. Angelo, close by the city.

Papal States.

(2) *Venice* was a commercial city, 1,000 years old, ruled by its nobles and possessing territory like ancient

Venice.   Rome, ruled for the benefit of its citizens
rather than its subjects.

(3) *Florence* was also a commercial republic, but not
governed by its nobles. It was a democratic republic,
Florence.   but one family of citizens—the Medici—had
grown by trade richer than the rest, and
usurped almost despotic power. It also possessed considerable territory.

(4) *Milan* was a State to which there were many rival
claims. The King of France, as Duke of Orleans, claimed
Milan.   it by inheritance from the last Duke of Milan. The King of Naples (and Spain through
him) also had a claim, and the Emperor of Germany
claimed it as having reverted to the Empire. Meanwhile
the *Sforza* family had possession, and kept it off and on
till 1512.

.(5) *Naples* was also a State to which there were rival
claims. Its nobles had usurped almost uncontrolled
power. The right to feudal sovereignty over it was dis-
Naples.   puted between the Counts of Anjou (France)
and the King of Arragon (Spain). The lat-
ter had long had possession, and it had descended to a
bastard branch of that house.

That the Popes were continually fomenting quarrels
between these Italian States and bringing 'barbarian'
princes to fight their battles on Italian soil, a few facts
will show.

Alexander VI. and Cæsar Borgia first stirred up
Venice and *Milan* against *Naples*. Then they invited
Charles VIII. of *France*, who in 1494 crossed the Alps,
overturned the Medici at Florence, and entered Naples
in 1495. Then in 1495 the *Pope, Venice,* and *Milan*
joined with Ferdinand of *Spain* in turning the *French*
out of Naples again.

In 1500 Louis XII. of France took Milan, and then he and Ferdinand of *Spain* jointly invaded *Naples*. But they quarrelled, and *Spain*, under Gonsalvo de Cordova, defeated the *French*, and so Ferdinand became King of Naples, and (having Sardinia and Sicily before) of the two Sicilies in 1505.

Papal politics the ruin of Italy.

In 1503 Julius II. became Pope, and devoted his ten years' reign to constant war. In 1509 he, *France*, *Spain*, and *Germany* formed the *League* of Cambray against *Venice*. But the robbers quarrelled on the eve of victory, and so Venice was not ruined.

In 1511 Louis XII. of *France* tried to get Henry VIII. of *England* to join him in deposing Julius II. But Julius succeeded in getting *England* and *Spain* and *Germany* to join his 'Holy League' against *France*.

After driving Louis XII. of *France* out of Italy, Julius II. died in 1513, and was succeeded by Leo X.

(b) Germany.

Next to Italy, Germany was furthest of all modern nations from having attained national unity. The German, or, as it called itself, 'the Holy Roman' Empire, was a power which belonged to the old order of things. Like the Pope of Rome, the Emperor considered himself as the head of Christendom. He called himself 'Cæsar,' and 'King of Rome;' and, as successor to the Roman Empire, which the Germans had conquered, claimed not only a feudal chieftainship over nations of German origin, but also a sort of vague sovereignty over all lands. As the Pope of Rome was the spiritual head, so the Emperor considered himself the 'temporal head of all Christian people.'

Had not yet attained national unity.

The Emperor claimed to be Cæsar and King of Rome.

Switzerland had indeed severed herself from the German Empire. England, Spain, and France had never properly belonged to it. But the French king had nevertheless sometimes sworn fealty to the Empire; and even Henry VIII. of England, when it suited his purpose (*i. e.* when he wanted to be Emperor!) took care to point out to the Electors that while his rival,

His claim to universal empire very shadowy.

Francis I. of France, was a foreigner, in electing an English Emperor, they would not be departing from the *German tongue.*

On other occasions he took care to insist that England, however Saxon in her speech, had never been subject to the Empire. So the claim to universal sovereignty was very shadowy indeed.

When a vacancy occurred, the new Emperor was elected under the 'Golden

How elected.

Bull' of 1356, by seven Prince Electors, viz.: [On the Rhine]. The three Arch-bishops of *Mayence, Treves,* and *Cologne,* and the Count Palatine of the Rhine. [On the Elbe]. The king of *Bohemia,* the Elector of *Saxony,* the Margrave of *Brandenburg.*

THE SEVEN PRINCE ELECTORS

The ceremony of coronation showed the feudal nature of the Empire. When elected, the Emperor attended high mass. Then the Archbishop of Mayence, as-

The feudal ceremony.

sisted by Cologne and Treves, demanded of him, 'Will you maintain the Catholic faith?' 'I will.' Then he demanded of his brother electors, 'Will you recognize the elected as

Emperor ?' 'So be it.' Then he was robed in the robes, girt with the sword, and crowned with the crown of Charlemagne. Then came the banquet. The King of Bohemia, in true feudal fashion, was the imperial cup-bearer; the Count Palatine carved the first slice from the roasted ox; the Duke of Saxony rode up to his stir-rups into a heap of oats, and filled a measure with grain for his lord; and lastly, the Margrave of Brandenburg rode to a fountain and filled the imperial ewer with water.

When elected, the Emperor had little real power in Germany; and, indeed, as time went on he seemed to have less and less.

Once large domains had belonged to the Emperor: some in Italy, some on the Rhine. But former emperors had lost or ceded the Italian estates to Italian nobles and cities during struggles with the Popes; while those on the Rhine *No imperial domains.* had been handed over to the Archbishops of Mayence, Treves, and Cologne, who were Electors, to secure votes and political support. For some generations there had been no imperial domains at all; not an inch of territory in Germany or Italy came to the Emperor with his impe-rial crown. The Emperor was therefore reduced to a mere feudal headship.

Nor had the Emperor, as feudal head, much power in Germany. He found it very hard to get troops or money from the German people. *Maximi-lian*, the reigning Emperor, was notoriously *Small imperial power.* poor, and declared that the Pope drew a hundred times larger revenue out of Germany than he did. He was a powerful sovereign in Europe because he was head of the Austrian house of Hapsburg, which was rising into great power in Europe by its alliances.

Already possessed of Austria and Bohemia, Maxi-

milian had married Mary of Burgundy, and the Netherlands. His son Philip thus was heir-apparent to those provinces as well as Austria.
Philip married Joanna, daughter of Isabella
of Spain; and so their son Charles became
heir to Spain also. Thus was the House of Hapsburg
pushing itself into power and influence. The German
Empire was the crowning symbol of their power rather
than the reason of it. In the case of Maximilian, it was
the power of Austria that made the German Emperor
great. By-and-by, as we shall see, when Charles V. of
Austria, Spain, and the Netherlands rises to
the Empire and becomes the most powerful
prince in Europe, it is by Spain, not Germany, that he
wields his still greater influence.

The Emperor Maximilian, of the Austrian House of Hapsburg.

Charles V.

The power of the Emperor was far less in Germany
than in his own domains, for in Germany his power was
checked by the Diet or feudal parliament of the Empire.
The Diet was a feudal, not a representative
parliament; *i. e.* only the Emperor's feudal
vassals had a claim to attend and vote in it.

The Diets.

The Diet met and voted in three separate houses:

1. The Electors (except the King of Bohemia, who
   had no voice except in the election of an Emperor).

2. The Princes, lay and ecclesiastical.

3. The Free Imperial Cities (*i. e.* those cities which
   held direct of the Emperor).

The Electors and Princes had most power. Only what
was agreed upon by them was last of all submitted to the
House of Cities. To secure the carrying out
of the decrees of the Diets, there had also
recently been some attempts at an organiza-
tion of the Empire. It was divided in circles for the

No power to enforce their decrees.

maintenance of order; but this, though plausible on paper, had little effect in reality, because the Diets had no real power to enforce their decrees.

Germany was, in fact, still under the feudal system—still divided up into petty lordships—more so than perhaps any other country; certainly more so than England, Spain, or France.

The feudal system still prevailed.

One reason for this was, as we have seen, that the German law of inheritance divided the lordships between the sons of a feudal lord on his death; so there was constant subdivision, and in consequence an ever-increasing host of petty sovereignties.

Subdivision of lordships by law of inheritance.

The mass of the feudal lords were petty and poor, and yet proud and independent, resisting any attempts of the powers above them, whether Emperor, or Diets, or Princes, to control them. They claimed the right of waging war; and, by their petty feuds, the public peace was always being broken.

Constant petty feuds.

They lived a wild barbarian life in times of peace (*i. e.* when not at feud with some neighbouring lord), devoted to the chase, trampling over their tenants' crops, scouring the woods with their retainers and their dogs. In times of war and feuds, with helmets, breastplates, and cross-bows they lay in ambush in the forests watching an enemy, or fell upon a train of merchants on the roads from some town or city with which they had a quarrel. They became as wild and lawless as the wolves.

Götz von Berlichingen (popularly known as 'Götz with the Iron Hand'), and Franz von Sickingen were types of this wild knighthood. They were champions of fist-law (faust-recht). They called it private war, but it was often plunder and pillage

Lawlessness of the knights.

by which they lived.   Götz was indeed more like the head of a band of robbers than anything else. He one day saw a pack of wolves fall upon a flock of sheep. 'Good luck, dear comrades,' said Götz, 'good luck to *us* all and everywhere!'   These lawless knights were indeed like wolves, and, just as much as the wild animals they hunted, belonged to the old order of things, which must go out to make way for advancing civilization.

The free towns of Germany were her real strength. The citizens were thrifty, earned much by their com-
The towns of   merce, spent little, and so saved much.
Germany.   Each city was a little free state (for they had mostly thrown off their feudal lords), self-governed, like a little republic, fortified, well stored with money in its treasury, a year's provisions and firing often stored up against a siege.   The little towns were of course de- pendent in part on the peasantry round, buying their corn, and in return supplying them with manufactured goods. But the bigger towns lived by a wider commerce, and held their heads above the peasantry. Above all, they hated the feudal lords, whose feuds and petty wars
Their leagues   and lawless deeds put their commerce in
for mutual   peril.   Two hundred years ago, sixty towns
defence.   on the Rhine had leagued themselves to- gether to protect their commerce. After that had come the league[1] of the Hanse Towns, chiefly in the North of Germany, but including Cologne and twenty-nine adja- cent towns, and aiming at defending commerce from robberies by land as well as piracy by sea.

They had to form these leagues because Germany was divided and without a real head—not yet a nation—

---

[1] See the Map of Commerce.

though all that was good and great in it was
sighing for more national life, for a central
representative power strong enough to maintain the public peace, but hitherto sighing
in vain, finding in her Emperor little more help than
Italy found in her Pope.

Want of a
central power
to maintain
the public
peace.

No class in Germany had suffered more from want of
a central power than the peasantry. They still were in
feudal serfdom. While in other countries,
where there was a well-established central
government, the lot of the peasantry had
improved and serfdom almost been got rid
of, here in Germany their lot had grown
harder and harder for want of it.

The con-
dition of the
peasantry
growing
harder and
harder for
want of a
central power.

The German peasant, or '*Bauer*,' was still a feudal
tenant. In many ways he was no doubt better off than
a labourer for wages. His house was no mere labourer's
cottage—it was a little farm. He had about him his
land and his live stock, his barn and his stack. Under
the same roof with his family his cows and pigs lay upon
their straw and he upon his bed. On the raised cooking
hearth the wood crackled under the great iron pot hung
on its rack from the chimney-hood above, while sauce-
pans and gridirons, pewter dishes and pitchers with their
pewter lids were hung upon the walls; the oak table and
coffee were heirlooms with his house and his land. In
mere outward comforts many a free peasant, working
for wages and having no land to till for himself, would
gladly have changed places with him; but behind all
was his thraldom to his feudal lord.

He had traditions of old and better days, when he was
far more free, when his services were not so hard and the
exactions of his lord not so great. But in
the fourteenth century the Black Death had

History of
the German
'Bauer.'

D

thinned the population of Germany and made labour
scarce. In other countries, where the law of the land
had fixed the amount of the services, and where
the influence of commerce had substituted money-
payments for services, this scarcity of labour strengthened
the peasant in his struggle for freedom. But in Germany,
where there was no law to step in, and where services
continued, the scarcity of labour was only likely to make
the lords insist all the more upon their performance; and
so they had encroached more and more on the peasants'
rights, enacted more and more labour from them, increased their burdens, robbed them more and more of
their common rights over the pastures, the wild game,
and the fish in the rivers, grown more and more inso-
lent, till the peasants in some places had sunk almost
into slavery. It was galling to them to have to work for
their lords in fine weather, and to have to steal in their
own little crops on rainy days. Small a thing as it
might be, perhaps it was still more galling to receive
orders on holidays to turn out and gather wild straw-
berries for the folks at the Castle. Hard, too, it seemed
to them when, on the death of a peasant, the lord's
agent came and carried off from the widow's home the
heriot or 'best chattel,' according to the feudal custom—
perhaps the horse or the cow on which the family was
dependent.

But however bad a pass things might come to, there
was no remedy—no law of the land to appeal to against
the encroachments of their lords. The Roman civil law had indeed been brought in
by the ecclesiastics, and the lords favoured
it because it tended to regard serfs as slaves. The serfs
naturally hated it because it hardened their lot. There
was no good in appealing to it. It was one of their

Rebellion
his only
remedy.

grievances. So the peasants of each place must fight it
out with their own lords. They must rebel or submit,
waiting for better days, if ever these should come!

(c) Spain.

Spain was destined to become the first power in
Europe. She rapidly grew into a united nation, and
during the era attained the highest point of $\quad$ Becoming
power and prosperity she ever reached; but $\quad$ the first
she fell soon after from the pinnacle on which $\quad$ Europe.
she then stood, and has never since risen again so high.

Ever since the conquest of Spain by the Goths and
Vandals, in the eighth century, it had been a feudal
nation; and, as in most other feudal coun- $\quad$ Power of the
tries, the power had got into the hands of $\quad$ nobles.
the feudal lords or nobles. But Spain was singular in
this, that it had passed under a long period of Mohammedan rule.

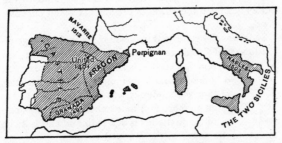

By the invasions of the Moors the feudal chiefs of
Spain had been driven up into the mountains of the
north, while probably the peasantry mostly $\quad$ Driven into
remained in the conquered country, subject $\quad$ the north by
to the Moors. By slow degrees the feudal $\quad$ the Moors.
chiefs reconquered the northern provinces till the Moors

retained only the rich southern provinces; and as bit after bit was reconquered by the nobles, it became a little
independent state under the feudal chief who reconquered it.

Already, however, there had grown up in Spain the
three kingdoms of Castile, Arragon, and Navarre, favoured by the influence of the towns.
Owing to the constant struggles going on
there had been for long no safety except
in the towns. These had further grown in
power and importance by trade and manufactures, and
had become little states—like little Venices— each with
its independent government.

Reconquest of Spain from the Moors, except Granada.

Both in Castile and Arragon the monarch was scarcely more powerful than the Emperor in Germany. His
power was controlled by the Cortes or parliament, at which met the nobles, deputies
from the towns, and clergy. And to the
Cortes belonged the power of levying taxes and enacting
laws.

Kingdoms of Castile and Arragon

Such was the state of things when, by the marriage of
Ferdinand of Castile to Isabella of Arragon (in 1481), all
Spain, except Navarre and Granada, was
united under one monarchy, and from this
time the tendency was for the throne to become more and more absolute. It was one
of the first objects of Ferdinand and Isabella
to extend the power of the monarchy.

united under Ferdinand and Isabella.

Spain becomes more and more absolute.

Spain had found, as the Germans had found, that
without some central power it was hard to keep the
peace, to protect trade and commerce, and to put down
robbery and crime. The cities had united in a ' Holy
Brotherhood' for this purpose, and Ferdinand sided with
them in this object. But what more than anything else

counteracted the feudal tendency to separate into little petty states, and to strengthen the national feeling and make it rally round the common centre of the throne, was the war long waged by Ferdinand, and at length successful, against the Conquest of Granada. last stronghold of the Moors in Granada. In 1492 Granada was taken, the 700 years' struggle ended, and the Moors driven forever out of Spain. Thus was all Spain (except the little state of Navarre, under shelter of the Pyrenees) united in one nation. The modern kingdom of Spain, thus formed, rose up at once to be one of the first powers of Europe.

We have already seen how Charles VIII. of France had been invited by Pope Alexander VI. to conquer Naples. As a bribe to keep Ferdinand (who had a rival claim on Naples) quiet while he went on this raid on Naples, he had ceded Ferdinand's policy to complete Spain. to Ferdinand the little state of *Perpignan*, on the Spanish side of the Pyrenees. Ferdinand was intent on the completion of the kingdom of Spain, and took the bribe. We shall soon find him (in 1512) obtaining possession of Navarre. In the meantime the result of the Italian wars was that he got hold of Naples; and having the islands of Sardinia and Sicily already, he became King of the 'Two Sicilies,' as well as of Spain.

Another fact added to the power of Spain. It was under Spanish auspices that Columbus discovered America. This not only threw the gold of the mines of Peru into the treasuries of Spain; it added another great laurel to her fame. It was Columbus. Spain that had driven the Moors out of Western Europe; it was Spain that enlarged Christendom by the discovery of the New World.

The foreign policy of princes in those days was very much influenced by the marriages they planned and effected for their children.

Ferdinand's first aim was to get all the Spanish Peninsula under the power of the Spanish Crown. So he married his eldest daughter to the King of Portugal, in hopes of some day uniting the two Crowns. This came to pass in the person of Philip II., the husband of the English Queen Mary.

His next policy was to ally himself with such foreign powers as would best help him to secure his ends. There were two reasons why he did not ally himself with France. France was his rival in Italy. He had fought with France for Naples, and meant to keep it. He also wanted Navarre to complete the Spanish kingdom. France claimed it also. The aim of Spanish foreign policy was, therefore, to work against France.

By the marriage of his daughter *Catherine* to the King of England, and *Joanna* to the heir of the rising Austrian House of Hapsburg, who held the Netherlands, and whose head, Maximilian I., was Emperor of Germany, he connected himself with the two powers who, like himself, were jealous of France—*England*, because part of France had so long been claimed as belonging to the English Crown—the *House of Hapsburg*, because France had got hold of part of Burgundy (which formerly belonged to the same Burgundian kingdom as the Netherlands).

And on the whole, though his schemes did not prosper in his lifetime, they did succeed in making Spain the first power in Europe during the next reign.

When Queen Isabella died, Joanna became Queen of

Castile. She, however, was insane, and her husband
Philip dying soon after, Ferdinand held the reins of
Castile in her name as Regent. On his death, in 1516,
Castile and Arragon were again united, under Charles
V., and Spain became greater than ever.

The domestic policy of Ferdinand and Isabella had
also for its object the consolidation of Spain   Domestic po-
under their throne. Their great minister   licy.
was Cardinal Ximenes, whose policy was to
strengthen the central power of the Crown by engaging
all Spain in a *national* war against the Moors, and by
strengthening the towns (or loyal element) at the expense of the feudal nobles (the disloyal element, in Spain
as elsewhere). The subjugation of the no-   Subjugation of
bles to the Crown was in a great measure   the nobles.
effected, and the Crown became more and more absolute.

Not content with driving out of Spain the last rem-
nant of the Mohammedan Moors, the Catho-   The Inquisi-
lic zeal of the king and queen and Ximenes   tion.
turned itself against the Jews and heretics. They founded
the '*Inquisition*' in Spain, which in a genera-   Banishment
tion burned thousands of heretics. They   of the Jews.
expelled, it is said, more than 100,000 Jews from their
Spanish homes. These first took refuge in Portugal, and
soon after, driven from thence, were scattered over
Europe.

But notwithstanding this zeal for the Catholic faith,
by which Ferdinand and Isabella earned the title of '*the
Catholic*,' there was no notion in the minds of Ximenes or
his royal master and mistress to sacrifice Spain to Rome.
They were as zealous in reforming the morals of the
clergy and monks as in rooting out heresy. They demanded from the Pope bulls enabling them to visit and

THE THREE DAUGHTERS OF FERDINAND AND ISABELLA, AND THEIR ALLIANCES.

FERDINAND King of Arragon m. ISABELLA Queen of Castile
[This marriage united Castile and Arragon under the Spanish crown.] (See Map of Spain, p. 34.)

ISABELLA m. Emanuel, King of Portugal,
[This marriage was intended to unite Spain and Portugal, and did do so under Philip II.]

JOANNA m. Philip of Austria
[Joanna was insane, and this marriage was intended to secure the union under the Spanish crown of the Austrian and Burgundian dominions. Philip, son of the Emperor Maximilian, who was head of the House of Hapsburg, inherited the Burgundian provinces (including the Netherlands) from his mother Mary of Burgundy. This marriage united Spain, Austria, and the Burgundian provinces under Charles V., who also became Emperor of Germany and King of Italy.]

CATHERINE m. Henry VIII. of England
[This marriage was intended to unite Spain and England in alliance against France. And so it did till the breach with Charles V., on his marriage with Isabella of Portugal instead of the Princess Mary. Whereupon Henry VIII. divorced Catherine, and this led to the revolt of England from Rome.]

Heir-apparent of Spain and Portugal, died young.

ISABELLA m. CHARLES V. Emperor of Germany
[Charles V. during the Spanish alliance with England was to have married the English Princess (afterwards queen) Mary. This marriage broke up the alliance between Spain and England.]

FERDINAND Archduke of Austria

PHILIP II. of Spain and Portugal m. MARY, Queen of England
[This marriage marked the reaction in England from the policy of Henry VIII.; the return to the Spanish alliance, and to allegiance to Rome. The reaction lasted till the death of Mary. Then under Elizabeth England again revolted from Rome. Whereupon Philip II. sent the ill-fated Spanish Armada against England. The Netherlands revolted from the Spanish rule of Philip II., and thus commenced the reaction against the supremacy of Spain in Europe.]

[A careful study of this page, and a reference back to it during the perusal of this volume, will be found a useful aid to the memory.]

reform the monasteries. They claimed the Independent policy to-wards Rome. right in many cases of appointing their own bishops. And when the scandals of Alexander VI.'s wicked reign came to their knowledge, they threatened to combine with other sovereigns in his ' *correction.*'

One other thing we must notice. The discoveries of Columbus, followed up by the conquest of Mexico and Peru, gave to Spain suddenly a colonial em- Colonial policy. pire to govern. Her colonies in the New World were in one sense the gem in her Crown. Her dreams of wealth in gold and silver were more than realized. To have extended *Christendom* into a new world seemed in itself a worthy exploit to the Catholic zeal of Queen Isabella. Her royal anxiety to convert the heathen inhabitants of the new-found lands to the Catholic faith was no doubt as genuine as her anxiety to root heresy out of Spain.

She sent out Catholic missionaries, but the selfishness of her Spanish colonists introduced slavery instead of Christianity. In these first Spanish colonies Slavery. was begun that cruel policy by which the native races were exterminated—worked to death—and then African negroes introduced to supply their place. The introduction of slavery, and its necessary feeder— the slave trade—was a blot upon the colonial policy, not only of Spain but of Christendom. It was essentially contrary to the genius of modern civilization, and we know how great a struggle has been needful in our own times to prevent its ruining the greatest of the colonies of the New World.

(*d*) *France.*

Machiavelli says, 'The kings of France are at this

time more rich and powerful than ever.'   So they were.

The dynasty of the *Capets*, which began before the time How all France had grown into one nation. of the Norman conquest of England and lasted down to the '*Louis Capet*' (Louis XVI.) who was put to death during the French Revolution, had now ruled France for about five hundred years.   But the France ruled by the first Capet

THE GROWTH OF FRANCE

was only the portion marked dark on the map.   It was as though the King of England had ruled only Yorkshire.   The rest of France was divided among the great Barons.

These Baronies, or '*Duchies*,' had gradually been absorbed into the kingdom.   The dates when they thus fell in are marked on the map.

Now if we look at France at the beginning of the France claimed Milan, and Naples also. new era, we shall see, from comparing the two maps, how she had grown, and how she claimed now not only all France, but Milan and Naples also.   She had, in fact, become the second great power in Europe, and by aiming to become the

FRANCE IN THE ERA

first, made herself the great rival of Spain.

What were the secrets of her growing power? As we have seen, Machiavelli said that Italy was weaker than either Spain or France, because the latter were each of them *united under one Crown.*

We have now to mark the reasons given by him why the Duchies of France had become united under the Crown. *This union of all France the result of—*

(1) The Crown was not elective, as in Germany, but hereditary in the royal family. *Crown heredi tary;*

(2) The *rule of inheritance* in France was not division among all the sons, but descent to the eldest son only. *primo- geniture;*

(3) Intermarriages with the royal family not only made the great Barons loyal to the throne, but sometimes united their Duchies to the Crown under one heir; *e. g.* the kings of France, as heirs of the Duchies of Anjou and Orleans, claimed both those Duchies and also their rights to Naples and Milan. *inter- marriage with the royal family.*

(4) The towns, as in Spain and elsewhere, had favoured the growth of the central power as the best means of freeing themselves from their old feudal lords. Most of them had long ago obtained charters of freedom, and now held only of the Crown. *The towns.*

The final struggle of the Crown with the great feudal Barons had been concluded just before the era commenced. It had been a hard struggle between Louis XI. and the Duke of Burgundy. The king had prevailed, and from that time the unity of France was settled. She had become powerful enough to hold her own against both internal and foreign foes. *Final struggle of the Crown with Bur- gundy.*

England had once claimed a great part of France, but

English con-
quests at
an end.

there was henceforth no real chance of her getting it back again. She could no longer find allies on French soil against France.

It is true that we shall find Henry VIII. still dreaming sometimes of reversing the decision of the 'hundred years' war' which had ended in the withdrawal of England from all France except the town of Calais; and we shall find Spain and England combining during the era more than once to crush France. But in reality the object of these wars we shall find to be not so much the dismemberment of France as opposition to the aggressive policy of Louis XII. and Francis I., and their invasions of Italy.

The hundred years' war with England had also tended to consolidate the French nation. It was a national and even popular struggle to turn out a foreign

The English
wars had
helped to unite
the nation, and
increase the
power of the
Crown:

foe. It necessitated the levying of national armies and the payment of national taxes. It did for France, to some extent, what the wars with the Moors did for Spain: it strengthened the central power of the Crown, and gave it a recognized place as natural head and leader of the nation, in peace as well as in war.

But the misfortune of France was that in outwardly becoming a great nation by uniting all the Duchies

but there were
seeds of dis-
union within.

under the Crown, and so enlarging the size of France on the map, sad mistakes were made, which prevented her growth in *internal unity*, which sowed the seeds of bitter feeling between classes, and ended in producing her Great Revolution.

We cannot note too carefully these fatal mistakes.

(1) The king got the power of levying taxes—the

'*taille*'—without the consent of the people. The 'Estates General,' or French Parliament, which had hitherto had a voice in matters of taxation, hereafter had none; the Crown became absolute.

(2) The king, successful in his war against England, henceforth out of these taxes kept a large standing army.

These things, said *Philip de Commines*, the contemporary French historian of Louis XI., 'gave a wound to his kingdom which will not soon be closed.'

He was right, for these two things kept classes apart and broke up the internal unity of France. To see how they did this, let us look at each class separately.

The nobility or *noblesse* of France were made into a permanently separate caste. In old times they paid no taille, because they gave their military services to the king in his wars. Now there was a standing army they were less and less needed as soldiers, yet their freedom from taxation remained. They were a privileged class, and intermarried with one another. Their estates went down to their eldest sons, but the younger sons, too, belonged to the noblesse. So they became a very numerous class, poor, but proud of their blood and freedom from taxes.

The *peasantry*, on the other hand, were the burdened class. In some respects they were much better off than the German peasantry. Very early in their history feudal serfdom had been abolished in the north of France, especially in Normandy; while in most parts their services in labour had been long ago changed into fixed rents, paid most often in corn, wine, or fruits. But their young crops still suf-

but paying
rents   fered from the lord's game. They still had
tolls and fees and heriots to pay, and forced
labour to give on the roads. They still looked up to the
feudal lord as to a master, and the lord down upon them
as born for service. There was an impassable barrier
of blood between the two classes. The Church added
and tithes   her claims—her tithes, as in other countries,
and the endless fees and money payments,
which made her so obnoxious. Bishops and abbots,
in France as in Germany, had large estates as well as
tithes, and so were landlords and princes as well as
priests, drawing, Machiavelli says, two-fifths of the
annual revenues of the kingdom into their ecclesiastical
coffers. Lastly came the extra burden of the taille,
growing with the military needs of kings who, having an
and taille.   army, and not content with turning out the
English and conquering refractory barons,
must needs lay claim to Milan and Naples, and invade
Italy.

Here is a picture drawn by the peasants themselves of
their hard lot, as they complained to the States General
on the accession of Charles VIII., and laid their grievances before the new monarch, hoping for a remedy
which never came.

'During the past thirty-four years troops have been
'ever passing through France and living on the poor
Their grie-   'people. When the poor man has managed
vances.   'by the sale of the coat on his back, after
'hard toil, to pay his taille, and hopes he may live out
'the year on the little he has left, then come fresh troops
'to his cottage, eating him up. In Normandy multi-
'tudes have died of hunger. From want of beasts men
'and women have to yoke themselves to the carts, and
'others, fearing that if seen in the daytime they will be

'seized for not having paid their taille, are compelled to
'work at night. The king should have pity on his poor
'people, and relieve them from the said tailles and
'charges.'

Alas! Charles VIII., instead of listening to their complaints, took to invading Italy! increasing their taille
and spilling more of their blood.

When to all this we add the consciousness that while
they, the much-enduring peasantry, were bearing their
increasing burdens, the noblesse were free from them,
can we wonder if the peasantry should learn to hate as
well as envy the nobles?

The middle class in order to escape the incidents of
the rural taxation more and more left the rural districts to
live in the towns. Not sharing the blood or The middle
the freedom from taille of the nobles, there class leave
was no mixing or intermarrying with them. for the country
They were of different castes. Neither did towns.
the men of the towns sympathize with the peasantry.
They had their taille to pay like the peasantry, but under
their charters they enjoyed privileges which the peasant
did not. They were merchants rather than manufactu-
rers. Some linen manufactures were carried on in
Brittany and Normandy, but mostly France was supplied
with goods from the looms of Flanders in exchange for
corn and wine. The towns were the markets in which
the products of the peasant were exchanged, and the
townsmen thus had the chance of throwing a part of
their burdens on their rural customers in the shape of
tolls and dues. While thus the noblesse grew prouder
and poorer, and the peasantry were more and more burdened, the middle classes in the towns grew richer and
more and more powerful.

Hence the gulf between different classes in France was

ever widening. The Crown was absolute and uncontrolled by any parliament, the noblesse a privileged caste, the middle class settling in the towns, while the poor peasantry were left to bear their burdens alone in the country. France had grown a big united country on the map, but looking within the nation, a state of things had begun which, if unreformed, was sure in the end to produce revolution, though it might not come yet.

Separation of classes the main vice in French polity.

In the meantime the first false steps of the absolute kings of France were those attempts at aggrandizement which led them to invade Italy and prove their strength in a long rivalship with Spain. To gratify a royal lust for empire and military glory they were ready to sacrifice the welfare of the French people.

Love of foreign wars the chief vice in her policy.

(*e*) *England.*

England had advanced further on the path of modern civilization than any other country.

The English people had long ago become a compact nation, with a strong central government, and with one law for all classes within it.

The English nation already formed.

England had passed under the feudal system, and, like other countries, had her separate feudal elements, needing to be blended into one compact whole. But happily in England this work had in good measure been done.

Her feudal nobles, especially since the wars of the Roses, had been thoroughly subdued under the central power. Early in her history the petty feudal lords had sunk into commoners. Unlike the noblesse of France, the nobility of England was not a separate caste. The younger sons of nobles

The nobility not a caste.

became commoners, while their title to nobility, as well as their estates, went to the eldest sons only.

England possessed a numerous and powerful middle class, and it was not, as in France, con-   Middle
fined to the towns. Landowners and yeo-   classes.
men in the country belonged to it, as well as
the citizens and merchants.

And whilst all classes, including the nobility, had been subjected to the central government, they had none of them been crushed and humbled. The   The Crown
Crown had not become absolute, as in   also subject to
France. It, too, was subject to the laws of   the laws.
the land.

The central power, or government, consisted of—

(1) the King, (2) the House of Lords, in which the nobility had seats; and (3) the House of Commons, where the representatives of the free landholders, and of the free citizens or burgesses, sat side by side.   The govern-
No law could be passed without the concur-   ment a consti-
rence of the Crown and both Houses of Par-   tutional
liament. And the laws so passed were bind-   monarchy.
ing alike on king, nobility, and commoners, *i. e.*, on the whole nation. Nor could the Crown levy taxes without the consent of Parliament. The government of England was a constitutional monarchy, and had long been so.

There was, however, still one class of people who were not altogether blended into the nation—the ecclesiastics or clergy. Bishops and abbots, because they were great landholders and peers of the realm, had seats in the House of Lords, just as in Germany   The ecclesias-
the ecclesiastical princes were Electors as   tics.
well as the lay princes. In this sense they were Englishmen. But the clergy in the main owed allegiance to

E

Ecclesiastics
not altogether
Englishmen.
Rome, and in spite of the Constitutions of
Clarendon, were still ruled by ecclesiastical
law and ecclesiastical courts, and resented
civil interference. So they were subjects of the great
Roman ecclesiastical empire rather than of England.
Their allegiance was at least divided between the Pope
and the king, and often they were really foreigners. The
The Pope drew
revenues from
England.
Pope at the same time drew large revenues
from England as well as the king. The ecclesiastical power was more under control,
and had been for long more restrained by law in England than anywhere else; but still the fact was that Rome
had ecclesiastical sway over England. And in England,
as elsewhere, the clergy and monks had got a large part
of the land into their hands—probably about one-third
of the land of England belonged to them, as well as
tithes from the whole.

The fact that there was one law of the land made by
King and Parliament, and ruling all classes in the realm
The peasantry
had got free
from feudal
servitude.
(except the clergy), had, more than anything
else, helped the peasantry to rise out of
feudal servitude. There was no peasantry
in Europe (except the Swiss) which had already so completely got out of it as the English.

It early became the law of the land in England that
the services of the peasant could not be increased by the
lord. What they had been by long custom they must
not exceed. Then, by the influence of commerce, money payments were early substituted for labor service.
So that people became used to money rents for land and
money wages for labour. The population of England had
increased very rapidly up to the fourteenth century. It
was then nearly twice what it was afterwards, because
the Black Death in 1349 swept away half of it in a few

months. This of course made labour scarce. In spite of all that the lords could do, and in spite even of Acts of Parliament passed to prevent it, there was a great rise in wages.

Under the feudal law the feudal tenants might not leave their land. But now more and more they went to the towns, where they could earn higher wages than by tilling the land. There was of course a struggle to prevent it, but aided by the towns, the process went on. The feudal lords tried to enforce the old services, which had become so much more valuable since the Black Death. The more they did, the more their tenants deserted the land and went to the towns. The peasantry kept up a kind of strike, which came to a climax in the rebellion under Wat Tyler in 1381. They were so far successful that fixed money payments became general instead of services, and by the time of Henry VII. feudal servitude or villenage was at an end in England.

Quite a new state of things had grown up. Owing to the growth of the woollen manufactures, and the demand for wool, sheep-farming had very much in- The present creased. Instead of a lot of little peasants' condition of the holdings, the large farms of the wealthy peasantry. sheep-owners often covered the country side. The masses of the people in England were more and more becoming a free people working for wages, while such tenants as remained on the land paid fixed money rents instead of services, and instead of being tied to the land were ejected from their holdings if they could not pay their rents. No doubt the masses of the people in England had their hardships to endure. They had suffered during the civil war of the Roses from anarchy and lawlessness and the ravages of armies. Soldiers disbanded after foreign wars disturbed the country. Small tenants

found it hard to compete with larger ones, and on failure
to pay their rents lost their farms very often. The number of ejections from the land added of course to the idle
vagrant population. Robbery was thereby increased,

Freedom did
not neces-
sarily make
them better
off.

and as both thieves and vagabonds were
hung, sometimes twenty might be seen
hanging from a single gibbet. All this
showed that there were evils at work—

many things needing reform—but the English pea-

They had no
share in the
government,
but there
was nothing
to prevent
their getting
it.

santry had earned by their past struggles
this great advantage: instead of being
servile tenants of feudal lords, they were
free subjects, protected by the law of the
land, though freedom did not necessarily
make them better off, but often the con-

trary. They had indeed as yet no share in making the
laws, but there was nothing in their blood or in the law
of England to prevent their rising by industry and thrift
into owners of land, and as such claiming a voice in the
government of their country.

Such was England when, after the wars of the Roses,
Henry VII. conquered at the Battle of Bosworth, and
ascended the throne in 1485.

Henry VII. was born an orphan, a few months after
the death of his father, Edmund Tudor, Earl of Rich-

Henry VII.

mond. He was an exile in Brittany while
the civil wars were raging in England. He
was twenty-six when the young princes were murdered,
and Richard III. usurped the throne. At once, under
the advice of Morton, Bishop of Ely, an attempt was

A Welshman,
and landed
in Wales.

made to dethrone in his favour the tyrant
Richard III. He was only twenty-eight
when, after landing at Milford Haven, and
winning at the Battle of Bosworth, he was proclaimed

king. His family (the Tudors) were Welsh, and so he had wisely landed in Wales. Belonging himself to the Lancastrian house, and in order to conciliate the Yorkists, he had taken an oath to marry, and afterwards married, Elizabeth of York, daughter of Edward IV., thereby in a way uniting the blood of the two rival factions. He was received with acclamation in London, and ascended a precarious throne. It is well to note how precarious it was. The four previous kings had all been violently dethroned— Henry VI. imprisoned and murdered, Edward IV. deposed and exiled, Edward V. murdered, Richard III. slain in the Battle of Bosworth. *The throne precarious.*

Henry VII. himself was a usurper, and, though he was king by Act of Parliament, there were other claimants to the throne. Two of them, generally thought to be impostors, invaded England, and tried to seize upon his throne. *Other claimants.*

The first of these, *Lambert Simnel*, called himself Edward, Earl of Warwick, and was supported by the Yorkist nobility, but defeated at the battle of Stoke in 1487. *Lambert Simnel.*

The other, *Perkin Warbeck*, professed to be the Duke of York, who with his brother, Edward V., was supposed to have been murdered by Richard III. He was supported by Edward IV.'s sister, the Duchess of Burgundy, by the kings of France and Scotland, who were continually plotting against Henry VII., and every now and then, when it suited his purpose, by Ferdinand of Spain. Perkin Warbeck was taken prisoner in 1497, and beheaded in 1499. *Perkin Warbeck.*

Henry VII.'s foreign policy was peace and alliance with Spain. We have seen that the foreign policy of Spain was alliance with *Henry VII.'s foreign policy.*

England against France. Henry VII. wanted peace. This alone could give him a chance of establishing himself firmly on his precarious throne. To get peace he allied himself with Spain. While both were infants the Prince of Wales was betrothed to the Princess of Spain, Catherine of Arragon. Ferdinand was a treacherous ally. He dragged Henry VII. into the war with France which ended in the annexation of Brittany to France.

Marriages with Catherine of Arragon.
And when it suited his purpose he threatened to dethrone Henry, and even offered Catherine of Arragon to the King of Scotland. At length, as years passed, the marriage of Prince Arthur to Catherine took place; but Prince Arthur soon after died. Then came negotiations for Catherine's marriage with Prince Henry (Henry VIII.), and on the death of his queen Henry VII. offered to marry his late son's widow himself! At length, in 1503, the contract for the marriage with the Prince Henry was signed, but as Henry was not yet of age it could be set aside if any other alliance suited him better.

It is well to mark how these royal marriages were merely a part of the foreign policy of princes, and that from the first there had been great lack of good faith as regards *this* marriage, on which so much of England's future history was to turn.

Henry VII.'s domestic policy was in the main wise.
Henry VII.'s domestic policy.
King and usurper as he was, he yet took great pains to conform to the law of the land. Instead of trying to make the crown absolute, he remembered he was a constitutional monarch, and could levy no taxes without consent of Parliament.

Still, though a constitutional monarchy, the government of England in Tudor times was not conducted just as it is now. Parliament did not sit every year as it does now. Nor were there as now a prime minister and a cabinet of min-

His position as regards Parliament.

isters representing the majority in Parliament, responsible to Parliament, remaining in office only so long as they can command a majority in Parliament, and giving place to another prime minister and cabinet as soon as they find themselves in a minority. The king had the reins of government much more in his own hands than the Crown has now. He chose his own ministers who were responsible to him alone. And as the regular annual revenues of the Crown were sufficient to pay for the ordinary expenses of government, and did not need voting by Parliament every year as they do now, it was only when he had a war on hand, or something extraordinary happened needing fresh taxes or laws, that it was needful for a Tudor king to call a Parliament.

The chief minister of Henry VII. was Cardinal Morton, a true Englishman, though an ecclesiastic. He was a man of large experience. He was in middle life when Henry was born. He was a privy councillor, and faithful adherent of

His minister, Cardinal Morton.

Henry VI. Edward IV. had made him his Lord Chancellor, and his executor. Richard III. had thrown him into prison, but he had escaped in time to plan the enterprise which proved successful at Bosworth Field, and to him Henry VII. owed his throne.

Under the influence of Morton Henry VII. on the whole did what the weal of England required.

With a strong hand he kept all classes subject to the laws of the land, quelled rebellion, and maintained internal peace and order. He was avaricious, but even in his most hard and unjust exactions he kept within the letter of the law.

Order maintained.

In order to keep the nobility in check he favoured the
Middle classes growth and power of the middle classes—
favoured. notably of the 'yeomen,' *i. e.* small landholders, and tenant farmers.

Thus he did much to conciliate the English nation
after the long civil wars. He also paved the way for
Paved the the union of England and Scotland by the
way for the marriage of his daughter Mary to the king
union of Eng-
land and Scot- of Scots. Being himself a Welshman, he
land. reconciled the Welsh to English rule. After
a struggle of 1,000 years they at length were satisfied
with union with England. Under the Tudor dynasty
Finally con- they ceased to feel themselves a conquered
ciliated the people, and though retaining their separate
Welsh. language, ceased to rebel from what they
no longer considered a foreign yoke.

To these claims of Henry VII. to English respect we
must add that, though not sagacious enough to patronize
And began Columbus, he did the next best thing in
England's sending out afterwards *Sebastian Cabot* to
colonial em-
pire. discover and claim for England a foothold
across the ocean which proved the beginning of those extensions of England in America in
which half the English people now dwell. Thus he was
the founder of England's colonial empire.

Of his later years we shall have to speak again. In
the meantime it may help to fix some of these facts on
our minds if we dwell a moment on his tomb.

'His corpse' (says the chronicler) 'was conveyed with
'funeral pomp to Westminster, and there buried by the
The tomb of 'good queen, his wife, in a sumptuous and
Henry VII. 'solemn chapel, which he had not long
'before caused to be builded.' He was
buried in a vault just big enough for himself and his

queen, under the pavement in the centre of that beautiful chapel which still bears his name, and in which, round this central tomb, so many Tudor and Stuart princes were afterwards laid. When Henry VII.'s vault was opened in 1689 there were found to be three coffins instead of two ! The third was discovered to be that of James I. To make room for it the wood had been stripped off the other two, leaving the inner lead coffins bare. The workmen engaged in this strange work were found to have quaintly scratched their names on the lead, with the date 1625.

In that tomb of Henry VII. lie, therefore, not only the heirs of the two English contending factions of York and Lancaster, and of the traditions of Wales, but also the Scotch monarch who, thanks to the policy of his great-grandfather, Henry VII., ascended the English throne and became the first king of Great Britain.

CHAPTER IV.

THE NEED OF REFORM AND DANGER OF REVOLUTION.

(a) *The Necessity for Reform.*

Now, after this review of the state of Christendom, it will be easy to see in what points it fell short of the demands of modern civilization and wherein therefore reform was needful.

We said that the first point towards which modern civilization specially tended was this, viz., the formation of compact nations living peaceably side by side, respecting one another's rights and freedom.

We have seen that the modern nations were fast forming themselves—that England, France, and Spain were already formed, but that Italy and Germany were lagging far behind in this matter.

Italy and Germany not yet united nations.

But none of the nations were living peaceably side by side, and respecting one another's rights. They were at constant war, sometimes under the leadership of the Pope, like a band of robbers, setting upon Venice, or Naples, or Milan; then quarrelling amongst themselves, and forming fresh leagues to drive one another out. Their foreign policy was aggressive and wofully wanting in good faith. This want of public peace and international morality was a crying evil. It disturbed commerce, and its worst result was that it inflicted terrible hardships on the masses of the people. The voice of the French peasantry was clear upon this point. Here then was need for reform.

The lack of international peace and justice.

The second great point aimed at by modern civilization was, that (looking *within* each nation) all classes of the people were to be alike citizens, for whose common weal the nation was to be governed, and who were ultimately to govern themselves.

Not only as yet had the masses of the people no share in the government of the nations of which they formed so large a part, but also they were very far from being regarded as free citizens, except in England, where in theory they were so, though perhaps not much so in practice. In Germany especially, the peasantry were still in feudal serfdom, and feeling their thraldom more keenly than ever. Here, again, was a necessity for reform.

The serfdom of the German peasantry still continued.

We have already seen that there was a necessity for

reform in that ecclesiastical system of Rome which opposed the free growth of the modern nations, and in the scholastic system so intimately connected with it, which was opposed to free thought, science, and true religion, and prevented the diffusion of the benefits of knowledge and education among the masses of the people. The ecclesiastical and scholastic systems needed reform.

Now the question for the new era was, whether the onward course of modern civilization was to be by a gradual timely reform in these things, or whether, reform being refused or thwarted, it was to be by revolution. The alternatives, reform or revolution.

Recognizing the necessity there was for reform, we have now to see the danger there was of revolution; how far and wide, in fact, the train was already laid, waiting only for the match to explode it.

(b) The Train laid for Revolution.

It will not seem strange, (1), that it was among the oppressed peasantry of Germany that the train was most effectually laid for revolution; or, (2), that when attempts had been made at revolution, they were aimed at the redress of both religious and political grievances. The train was laid among the German peasantry.

The ecclesiastical grievances of the peasantry were as practical and real as those involved in feudal serfdom. The peasant's bondage to the priests and monks was often even harder than the bondage to his feudal lords. It was not only that he had tithes to pay, but after paying tithes, he still had to pay for everything he got from priests and church. That religion which should have been his help and comfort was become a system of extortion and fraud. Their ecclesiastical as well as feudal grievances.

These are the words of a contemporary writer (Juan
de Valdez, the brother of the secretary of the Emperor
Charles V.), himself a Catholic, and well acquainted with the condition of things in
Germany: 'I see that we can scarcely get
'anything from Christ's ministers but for money; at bap-
'tism money, at bishoping money, at marriage money,
'for confession money—no, not extreme unction without
'money! They will ring no bells without money, no
'burial in the church without money; so that it seemeth
'that Paradise is shut up from them that have no money.
'The rich is buried in the church, the poor in the church-
'yard. The rich man may marry with his nearest kin,
'but the poor not so, albeit he be ready to die for love of
'her. The rich may eat flesh in Lent, but the poor may
'not, albeit fish perhaps be much dearer. The rich man
'may readily get large indulgences, but the poor none, be-
'cause he wanteth money to pay for them.'

Contempo-
rary testi-
mony.

We must remember, too, how galling to the peasant
was the payment of the large and small tithes. These
words were written in England, but they will serve for
all Europe:

'They have their tenth part of all the corn, meadows,
'pasture, grass, wood, colts, calves, lambs, pigs, geese,
'and chickens. Over and beside the tenth
'part of every servant's wages, wool, milk,
'honey, wax, cheese, and butter; yea, and
'they look so narrowly after their profits that the poor
'wife must be countable to them for every tenth egg, or
'else she getteth not her rights at Easter, and shall be
'taken as a heretic.'

Another testi-
mony.

Can we wonder that the peasants should rebel against
this? and that in Germany, where both feudal and ecclesiastical oppression was so galling, they should rebel

against both, and mix the two together in their minds, demanding in one breath both religious and political freedom? Surely there was reason in it.

As early as the fourteentḥ century the Swiss peasants in the Forest Cantons had rebelled and thrown off the yoke of their Austrian feudal lords, and when the latter joined in a common cause against them, the Swiss were victorious in the battle of Morgaṛten, 1315. The Swiss had formerly belonged to the German Empire, and had the Empire done justice between them and their lords, ṭhey would have been glad enough to remain free peasants of the Empire; but as the Empire helped their lords instead of theṃ, they threw off the yoke of the Empire. They were soon joined by other neighboring cantons, and their flag, with its white cross on a red ground, became the flag of a new nation, the Swiss confederacy, with its motto, 'Each for all, and all for each'—a nation of free peasants, letting out their sons as soldiers to fight for pay, and, alas, not always on the side of freedom!

Between 1424 and 1471 the peasants of the Rhætian Alps did the same thing. Oppressed and insulted by their lords they burned their castles and threw off their yoke, and thus was formed the Graubund, in imitation of the Swiss confederacy, but separate from it.

Referring to the map '*Serfdom and Rebellions against it*,' we mark these two Swiss republics on it as the region where rebellion had met with success. It was no doubt their mountains which helped the Swiss peasants to success and independence. Their battles were little Marathons. At Morgarten 1,300 Swiss won the day against 10,000 Austrian troops. Their Alps were their protection.

We mark next the region where the rebellion against

Successful rebellion of the Swiss, 1315.

and the peasants of the Graubund, 1441-71.

Rome and the Empire, which followed in Bohemia upon

Unsuccess-
ful rebellion
of the Lol-
lards and
Hussite
wars, 1415–
1436.

the preaching of Wiclif and martyrdom of
Huss, had been, after a long reign of terror,
and the Hussite wars (1415-1436), quelled in
blood. Hussite doctrines were indeed still
held by the people, and by the treaty of
Basle in some sense tolerated; but this, nevertheless, was the region where rebellion, springing out
of the last era of light and progress, had been crushed
to rise no more.

Now we have got to mark where, in connexion with
the new era, there were signs, as we have said, that a
train was laid for a coming revolution.

The John the Baptist of the movement was *Hans Bo-
heim*, a drummer, who had appeared in 1476 in Franco-

Threats of
Rebellion in
Franconia in
1476.

nia, on the Tauber, a branch of the Maine.
He professed to be a prophet, to have had
visions of the Virgin Mary, and to be sent by
her to proclaim that the Kingdom of God was at hand,
that the yoke of bondage to lords spiritual and temporal
was coming to an end, that under the new kingdom there
were to be no taxes, tithes, or dues; all were to be
brethren, and woods, and waters, and pastures were to be
free to all men. A crowd of 40,000 pilgrims flocked to
hear the prophet of the Tauber till the Bishops of Wurz-
burg and Maintz interfered, dispersed the crowd and
burned the prophet. He was but a sign of the times—a
voice crying in the wilderness! But his cry was one
which found a response in the hearts of the peasantry—
freedom from the yoke of their feudal and spiritual lords,
and the restoration of those rights which in ancient days
had belonged to the community. This was the cry of
the peasantry for many generations to come.

The next was a much more formidable movement, viz.,

that named from the banner borne by the The 'Bund-
peasantry, the *Bundschuh*, or peasant's clog. schuh'

While the peasants in the Rhætian Alps were gradually throwing off the yoke of the nobles and forming the
Graubund, a struggle was going on between in Kempten,
the neighbouring peasantry of Kempten (to 1492.
the east of Lake Constance) and their feudal lord, the
Abbot of Kempten. It began in 1423, and came to an
open rebellion in 1492. It was a rebellion against new
demands not sanctioned by ancient custom, and though
it was crushed, and ended in little good to the peasantry
(many of whom fled into Switzerland), yet it is worthy
of note because in it for the first time appears the banner
of the Bundschuh.

The next rising was in Elsass (Alsace), in 1493, the
peasants finding allies in the burghers of the towns
along the Rhine, who had their own grie- In Elsass,
vances. The *Bundschuh* was again their 1493.
banner, and it was to Switzerland that their anxious eyes
were turned for help. This movement also was prema-
turely discovered and put down.

Then, in 1501, other peasants, close neighbours to
those of Kempten, caught the infection, and in 1502,
again in Elsass, but this time further north, Both again in
in the region about Speyer and the Neckar, 1501-2.
lower down the Rhine, nearer Franconia, the *Bundschuh* was raised again. It numbered on its recruit
rolls many thousands of peasants from the country
round, along the Neckar and the Rhine. The wild
notion was to rise in arms, to make themselves free,
like the Swiss, by the sword, to acknowledge no superior but the Emperor, and all Germany was to join the
League. They were to pay no taxes or dues, and commons, forests, and rivers were to be free to all. Here

again they mixed up religion with their demands, and
'Only what is just before God' was the motto on the
banner of the *Bundschuh.* They, too, 'were betrayed,
and in savage triumph the Emperor Maximilian ordered
their property to be confiscated, their wives and children
to be banished, and themselves to be quartered alive.
It would have been suicide on the part of the nobles to
fulfil orders so cruel on their own tenants. They would
have emptied their estates of peasants, and so have lost
their services, for the conspiracy was widely spread.
Few, therefore, really fell victims to this cruel order of
the Emperor. The ringleaders dispersed, fleeing some
into Switzerland and some into the Black Forest. For
ten years now there was silence. The *Bundschuh* banner was furled, but only for a while.

In 1512 and 1513, on the east side of the Rhine, in
the Black Forest and the neighbouring districts of Würtemberg, the movement was again on foot
on a still larger scale. It had found a leader
in *Joss Fritz.* A soldier, with commanding presence, and great natural eloquence,
used to battle, hardship, and above all, patience, he
bided his time. He was one of the fugitives who had
escaped being 'quartered.' He hid himself for years
in places where he was unknown, but never despaired.
At length, in 1512 he returned to his own land, settled
near Freiburg, and began to draw together again the
broken threads of the Peasants' league. He got himself appointed forester under a neighbouring lord, talked
to the peasants in the fields, or at inns and fairs, and
held secret meetings at a lonely place among the forests
in the dusk of evening. There he talked of the peasants' burdens, of the wealth of their ecclesiastical op-
pressors, of the injustice of their blood being spilled in

About the
Black Forest
1512–13,
under Joss
Fritz.

the quarrels of lords and princes, how they were robbed
of the wild game of the forest, and the fish in the rivers,
which in the sight of God were free, like the air and the
sun, to all men, how they ought to have no masters but
God, the Pope, and the Emperor. Lastly, he talked to
them of the *Bundschuh*. They went to consult their
priest, but Joss had talked over the priest to his side,
and he encouraged the movement. Then they framed
their articles, and Joss defended them out of the Bible.
ꞌThey were first to seek the sanction and aid of the Emperor, and if he refused to help them then they would
turn to the Swiss.

There was a company of licensed beggars who
tramped about the country with their wallets, begging
alms wherever they went—a sort of guild, with elected
captains. This guild Joss took into his confidence.
They were his spies, and through them he knew what
watches were kept at city gates, and through them he
kept the various ends of the conspiracy going. His plans
were now all laid. He wanted nothing but the *Bundschuh*
banner. He got some silk and made a banner—blue,
with a white cross upon it. The white cross was the
Swiss emblem. Some of his followers would have preferred the eagle of the Empire. But how was the *Bundschuh* to be added? What painter could be found who
would keep the secret? Twice he tried and was disappointed, and all but betrayed. At length, far away on
the banks of the Neckar, he found a painter, who
painted upon it the Virgin Mary and St. John, the Pope
and the Emperor, a peasant kneeling before the cross, a
Bundschuh, and under it the motto 'O Lord, help the
righteous.' He returned with it under his clothes, but
ere he reached home the secret was out. Again the
League was betrayed. A few days more and the ban-

ner would have been unfurled. Thousands of peasants were ready to march, but now all was over, the whole thing was out, and Joss Fritz, with the banner under his clothes, had to fly for his life to Switzerland. Everything was lost but his own resolution. Those conspirators who were seized were put to torture, hung, beheaded, and some of them quartered alive.

But Joss Fritz was not disheartened. He returned after a while to the Black Forest, went about his secret errands, and again bided his time.

In 1514 the peasantry of the Duke Ulrich of Würtemberg rose to resist the tyranny of their lord, who had ground them down with taxes to pay for his reckless luxury and expensive court. The same year, in the valleys of the Austrian Alps, in Carinthia, Styria, and Crain, similar risings of the peasantry took place, all of them ending in the triumph of the nobles.

In 1514 in Würtemberg and the Austrian Alps.

To defend themselves against such risings a league had been formed among the nobles of the whole district to the north of Switzerland, called the *Swabian League*, and a proclamation was issued that ' Since in the land of Swabia, and all ' over the Empire, among the vassals and poor people ' disturbances and insurrections are taking place, with ' setting up of the standard of the Bundschuh and other ' ensigns against the authority of their natural lords and ' rulers, with a view to the destruction of the nobles and ' all honourable persons, the noble and knightly orders ' have therefore agreed, whatever shall happen, to sup-' port each other against every such attempt on the part ' of the common man.'

The Swabian League against the peasants.

This brings forcibly into view again the fatal vice in the policy of feudal Germany—want of the consolidation

of the German people into a compact nation. Far and wide the train was laid for future revolution.
For here were the peasantry of Germany ap-
pealing helplessly to some higher power to
protect them from the oppression of their
feudal lords, conspiring for a general rebellion for lack of it, and debating whether on the flag of the
Bundschuh they should paint the eagle of the Empire or
the white cross of the Swiss republic.   Here on the
other hand were the nobles and knightly orders conspiring by the sheer force of their combined swords to
crush these ' attempts on the part of the common man.'
The crying need of both was for a German nation—a
commonwealth—with a strong central power or government to hold the sword of justice between them, settling
their disputes by the law of the land for their common
weal.   For lack of this there was rebellion and bloodshed.
These risings of the peasantry were crushed for a while,
but Joss Fritz was only biding his time, and meanwhile
let us bear in mind where, how far and wide over Central Europe, the train was laid, waiting only for the
match to ignite it.

It is well to look once more on the map of serfdom, to
fix these revolutionary localities in our mind, and before
we pass away from them to mark how they lie, *not* in
the region of darkest shadow, where serfdom was most
complete—wheie a conquered Slavonian peasantry were
in bondage too complete for rebellion—nor in the region
of the crushed Hussite rebellions ; *but* in those regions
next to the countries where serfdom had obtained least
hold, and had passed away ; above all, in The train laid out where serf-dom was at its worst, but where freedom was nearest in sight.
those mountain regions where the traditions
of ancient freedom had lived the longest,
where the spirit of the people was least subdued, and where the close neighbourhood of

their fellow mountaineers of Switzerland kept an example of successful rebellion ever before their eyes. We may see in this way most clearly how these peasants' rebellions were not isolated phenomena, but parts of a great onward movement beginning centuries back, which had already swept over England and France, and freed the peasants there, and now, in this era, had Germany to grapple with. Whether it was destined to be at once successful or not we shall see in this history, but we may be sure it was destined to conquer some day, because we cannot fail to recognize in it one of the waves of the advancing tide of modern civilization.

PART II.
THE PROTESTANT REVOLUTION.

CHAPTER I.

REVIVAL OF LEARNING AND REFORM AT FLORENCE.

(a) *The Revivers of Learning at Florence.*

THE story we have now to tell begins at Florence. Florence, as we have already noted, was a republic, but The Republic of Florence. differing from other Italian republics in this: that while in others the nobles held power, here in Florence, for some generations, the nobles had been dethroned. The people had got the rule into their own hands; and so far had they carried their distrust of the nobles, that no noble could hold office in the city unless he first enrolled himself as a simple citizen. Florence had long been a great commercial city, and the public spirit of her citizens had helped to make her prosper-

ous. Never had she been more prosperous than in the
early days of her democracy. But every now and then
there were troubled times; and in such times, more than
once or twice, a dictator had been chosen. Sometimes
even a foreign prince had been made dicta-   Power in the
tor for a stated number of years. At length   hands of the
                                                 Medici.
power had fallen into the hands of the
wealthier families of citizens, and the chief of these was
the family of the Medici.

Cosmo de' Medici was for many years dictator. His
great wealth, gained by commerce, placed him in the
position of a merchant prince. His virtues,   Cosmo,
and patronage of learned men and the arts,   1389-1464.
made him popular; and his popularity paved the way
for the proud position held by his grandson, 'Lorenzo
the Magnificent.'

Lorenzo de' Medici (of whose times we are to speak)
had followed in Cosmo's footsteps, and had got into his
single hand the reins of the state. He had   Lorenzo de'
set aside the double council of elected citi-   Medici,
                                                1448-1492.
zens, and now ruled through a council of
seventy men chosen by himself. His court was the
most brilliant and polished of his time, but in the background of his magnificence there was always this dark
shadow—he held his high place at the expense of the
liberties of the people of Florence.

There was, however, much in his rule to flatter the
pride of the Florentines.

Under the Medici, Florence had become the 'Modern
Athens.' Their genius and wealth had filled it with
pictures and statues, and made it the home   Florence the
of artists and sculptors. At this very mo-   Modern
                                              Athens.
ment, in Lorenzo's palace and under his
patronage, was young *Michael Angelo*, ere long to be the

greatest sculptor and one of the greatest painters of Italy.

Michael Angelo.

Learning also, as well as art, had found a home at Florence. The taking of Constantinople by the Turks having driven learned men into Italy, here at Florence, and elsewhere in Italy, the philosophy of Plato was taught by men whose native tongue was Greek. Cosmo de' Medici founded the '*Platonic Academy,*' and *Ficino,* who was now at the head of it, had been trained up under his patronage.

The Platonic Academy.

Ficino.

Politian (Poliziano), the most brilliant and polished Latin poet of the day, was always at the palace, directing the studies of Lorenzo's children, and exchanging Greek epigrams with learned ladies of the court. To this galaxy of distinguished men had recently been added the beautiful young prince, *Pico della Mirandola,* regarded as the greatest linguist and most precocious genius of the age. At twenty-three he had challenged all the learned men of Europe to dispute with him at Rome; and some of the opinions he advanced being charged with heresy, he had taken refuge at the court of Lorenzo, who gave him a villa near his own and Politian's, on the slope of the mountain overlooking the rich valley of the Arno and the domes and towers of Florence. What these three friends—Ficino the Platonist, Politian the poet, and Pico, their young and brilliant companion— were to each other, let this little letter picture to us.

Politian, 1454–1494; and Pico della Mirandola, 1463–1494.

Politian writes to Ficino, and asks him to come.

'My little villa is very secluded, it being embosomed among woods, but in some directions it may be said to overlook all Florence. Here Pico often steals in upon me unexpectedly from his grove of oaks, and draws me away with him from my hiding-place to partake of one of his pleasant suppers—temperate, as you know well, and brief, but always seasoned with delightful talk and wit. You will, perhaps, like better to come to me, where your fare will not be worse, and your wine better—for in that I may venture to vie even with Pico.'

Add to this picture the brilliance of Lorenzo's court, and what a fascinating picture it is!

This little knot of men at Florence, and others in Italy, were at work at what is called the 'Revival of Learning.' These revivers of learning are often spoken of as 'the *Humanists.*' They were dig- The Revival of Learning. ging up again, and publishing, by means of the printing-press, the works of the old Greek and Latin writers, and they found in them something to their taste much more true and pure than the literature of the middle ages. After reading the pure Latin of the classical writers they were disgusted with the bad Latin of the monks; after studying Plato they were disgusted with scholastic philosophy. Such was the rottenness of Rome that they found in the high aspirations of Plato after spiritual truth and immortality a religion which seemed to them purer than the grotesque form of Semi-pagan Christianity which Rome held out to them. tendencies of the They could flatter the profligate Pope as all revival of but divine in such words as 'Sing unto Six- learning. tus a new song,' but in their hearts some of them scoffed, and doubted whether Christianity be true and whether there is a life after death for mankind.

(b) The great Florentine Reformer, Girolamo Savonarola.

These were the revivers of learning. But suddenly there arose amongst them quite another kind of man—a religious Reformer. He came like a shell Girolamo Sa- in the midst of tinder, and it burst in the vonarola, 1452 –1498. midst of the Platonic Academy. The name

of this Florentine Reformer was *Girolamo Savonarola.*
He too was a learned man, meant by his father to be a
doctor, but being of a religious turn of mind he had
chosen to become a monk. Finding from study of the

Becomes a re-
ligious re-
former.

Scriptures how much both the Church and
the world needed reform, he became a Reformer. In 1486 he commenced preaching
against the vices of popes, cardinals, priests and monks,
the tyranny of princes, and the bad morals of the people, calling loudly for repentance and reformation. In
1487 he preached at Reggio. There young Pico heard
him, and, taken by his eloquence, invited him to Florence. In 1490 he came to the convent of St. Mark,
which was under the patronage of the Medici. Crowds
came to hear him; shopkeepers shut up their shops

Made prior of
St. Mark at
Florence.

while he was preaching. He became the
idol of the people. In 1491 he was made
Prior of San Marco, and when asked to do
customary homage to the patron for this high appointment he refused, saying ' he owed it to God, and not to
Lorenzo de' Medici ! '

Innocent VIII. had now succeed Sixtus IV. as Pope,
and his natural son had married Lorenzo's daughter.
The Pope in return had made Lorenzo's son John (afterwards Leo X.), a boy of thirteen, a cardinal! When
Savonarola thundered against ecclesiastical scandals and
the vices of the Pope, Lorenzo naturally did not like it.
He sent messages to the preacher, exhorting him to use
discretion. ' Entreat him,' replied the Reformer, ' in my
name, to repent of his errors, for calamities from on high
impend over him and his family.' The bold Reformer

Stirs up in the
people the
spirit of reform
and freedom.

went on with his preaching, denouncing judgments upon Italy and Rome. A marked impression was soon visible in the morals of the

people of Florence. More and more he became their
natural leader. Lorenzo tried to keep himself popular by
fêtes and magnificent festivals. But gradually influential citizens, who still longed for the old republic and
ancient liberty, attached themselves to Savonarola. In
1492 Lorenzo de' Medici died. The Re- Death of
former had been sent for, and was with him Lorenzo and
at his death. It was rumoured that he demanded of the
dying man, as a condition of absolution, that he should
restore to Florence her ancient liberties. Innocent VIII.
This year Innocent VIII. too died; and in
1493 the wicked reign of Alexander VI. and his son
Cæsar Borgia began. While they were plotting to bring
over Charles VIII. of France to scourge Italy, Savonarola mixed up with his denunciations against the evils
of the times prophecies of impending woes upon Florence. Then came the armies of France; The French
friendly relations between the French and invasion.
The Medici
the Florentines; the expulsion of the Medici, expelled. The
by their aid, from Florence; the formation republic re-
stored.
of a republic, under the advice of Savonarola. He declined to hold any office, but his spirit ruled supreme.
Convents were reformed, and the study of the Bible in
the original language made a part of the Savonarola's
duty of the monks. Schools for the educa- reforms.
tion of the children of the people were founded; and
Savonarola went on with his preaching, denouncing the
wickedness of the Church and demanding reform.

In 1495 Pope Alexander VI. thought it was time to
stop so dangerous a preacher. He cited him to Rome,
but the people would not let him go. He offered to make
him a cardinal as the price of his loyalty to Rome,
but he publicly replied that the only red hat to which he
aspired was one red in the blood of his own martyrdom.

Had Savonarola died in 1495, his name would have gone down to posterity as that of a reformer singularly zealous, noble, patriotic, judicious, and practical in his aims and conduct. But men are not perfect. The zealous brain is apt to take fire, and enthusiasm is apt to become fanatical. So it was with Savonarola. Both he and the people gave way to excitement. When the time of Carnival came, they dragged their trinkets, pictures, immoral books, vanities of all kinds, into the public square, and made a great bonfire of them. The excitement of the people reacted on the prophet who had raised it. In his later years (he lived only to the age of forty-seven), he prophesied more wildly than ever, thought he saw visions, and did fanatical things which marked a brain fevered and unbalanced. Be it so; we are not therefore to forget to pay homage to the man who, even in these later years, was bold enough to put the Borgian Pope to well-merited shame, and to denounce his vices, regardless alike of his bribes or his threats. That the Pope was powerful enough at length to put him to silence by imprisonment, to make him confess his heresies by torture, and on his return to them when the torture was removed, to silence him for ever by a cruel death, did but cast the halo of martyrdom around his heroism and make his name immortal. He was strangled and burned at Florence by order of the Pope in 1498—by order of that Pope who had himself committed murder and sacrilege and unheard-of-crimes, and who five years after died of the poison prepared, as was said, for another!

He becomes fanatical.

Is martyred by order of the Pope Alexander VI.

(c) *Savonarola's Influence on the Revivers of Learning.*

Lorenzo had died in 1492, and Savonarola, as we have said, was present at his death-bed. Pico, who had in-

vited him to Florence, became a devout dis- His influence
ciple of Savonarola, and after three years of over Pico.
pure and childlike piety, remarkably free Politian, and
from fanaticism, died in 1495. Just as Charles Ficino.
VIII. was entering Florence, Pico was buried in the
robes of Savonarola's order and in the church of St.
Mark. Politian died in the same year; he, too, desired
to be buried in the robes of Savonarola's order. Ficino
was carried away by the preaching of the Reformer for a
while, but was disgusted with the fanaticism of his later
years. He died a Platonist, hardly sure whether Christianity be true or not, and this characteristic story is told
about his death. He and a friend made a solemn bar-
gain with each other that whichever died first should, if
possible, appear to the other and tell him whether indeed
there be a life after death. Ficino died first, and is said
to have appeared to his friend, exclaiming, 'Oh! Michael!
Michael! it is all true!' Whether the story be true or
not, it shows exactly the state of mind the Neo-Platonist
philosophers were in.

(d) *Niccolo Machiavelli.*

For some time after Savonarola's death Florence was
governed by a Council of Ten, by whom was chosen as
Secretary of State one of the most remark- Niccolo Ma-
able men of the time, *Niccolo Machiavelli*, chiavelli
the historian from whose writings we have 1469-1527.
several times quoted. He was, perhaps, the keenest
diplomatist that ever lived. Schooled in the lying politics of Italy, while Cæsar Borgia and Alexander VI.
were plotting and counter-plotting with all the States of
Italy and Europe, he conducted the foreign diplomacy
of the Republic of Florence till 1512, when under Julius
II. the French were driven out of Italy and the sons of

Lorenzo de' Medici re-established in power. The Florentines then lost their freedom of self-government for ever, and Machiavelli found himself an exile. In the retirement of a hidden country life he wrote his great 'The Prince.'   work, 'The Prince.' Its object was to win a way back for its author to political life by convincing the Medici that though he had served under their enemies, he could do them service if they employed him. It answered its purpose. Written in a wicked, lying age, 'The Prince' reflected its vices. Its author made no pretence of a higher virtue than Borgias and Medici would appreciate. He did not scruple to advocate lying whenever it would pay; force and fraud whenever it would succeed; tyranny, if needful to keep a tyrant on his throne; murder and bloodshed as a means of obtaining an end. This was what professedly Christian popes had been doing of late. Machiavelli by putting these maxims into a scientific form in 'The Prince' did but give them a sort of personality. He became, as it were, the demon of politics, and the unchristian policy of the times became known to after ages as 'Machiavellian.'

CHAPTER II.

THE OXFORD REFORMERS.

*(a) The Spirit of Revival of Learning and Reform is
carried from Italy to Oxford.*

THERE were, as we have seen, two distinct movements at Florence in favour (1) of the *Revival of Learning*, and (2) of *Religious Reform*. The distinction and also the connexion between these movements must be marked with care.

The revival of the old classical Latin and Greek authors, by making men prefer Plato to the schoolmen dealt a blow at the scholastic system, and even tended towards a rejection of Christianity.

The spirit of religious reform was, on the other hand, a revival of earnest Christian feeling against the scandals of the Church and the irreligion of the age. It was in some sense caused by the revival of learning, for amongst the ancient literature which was revived were the Scriptures and the works of the early Church fathers; and the study of these in their original languages opened men's minds to the need of reform. It also set them against the scholastic theology, and so it came to pass that the spirit of religious reform in its turn dealt a blow against the scholastic system.

When the spirit which sought the revival of learning joined itself with that of religious reform, it produced reformers who aimed at freeing men's minds from the bonds of the scholastic system, at setting up Christ and his apostles instead of the schoolmen as the exponents of what Christianity really is, and lastly at making real Christianity and its golden rule the guide for men and nations, and so the basis of the civilization of the future.

So to some extent it had been in Italy. The revival of learning had produced, not only the Platonic Academy, but also the great Florentine Reformer; and Savonarola, with his fiery religious zeal, had been more than a match for the pagan tendencies of the Platonic Academy. Pico especially, and in part Ficino, had united religious feelings with a love of the Platonic philosophy. Savonarola himself had united a love of letters and zeal for education

The movement crushed at Florence. with his spirit of religious reform. But the movement at Florence was now thoroughly crushed. We must look elsewhere for its further development till it becomes a power all over Europe.

As in the fourteenth century the movement begun by Wiclif in England was carried into Bohemia by the inter-change of students between the Universities of Oxford and Prague, so this movement, begun in Italy, was soon carried by students from Florence to Oxford, and from thence it took a fresh start.

Revivers at Oxford.

During the lifetime of Lorenzo de' Medici several Oxford students, amongst whom were *Grocyn* and *Linacre*, went to complete their studies in Italy. Linacre was made tutor or fellow-student of Lorenzo's own children (one of whom was afterwards Pope Leo X.). They returned to Oxford to revive there the study of the Greek language and literature. Linacre afterwards became tutor to Arthur Prince of Wales, and physician to Henry VII.

Grocyn and Linacre go to Italy and return to Oxford.

Another Oxford student—*John Colet*—went to Italy after Lorenzo's death and the French invasion of Italy, and while Savonarola was virtually head of the Republic at Florence, also while the scandals of Rome's worst Pope, Alexander VI., and Cæsar Borgia, were in everyone's mouth. He caught the spirit, not only of the revival of learning, but also of religious reform, and, combining the two, became on his return to Oxford the beginner of a movement at Oxford which was to influence Europe.

John Colet does the same. Colet unites the spirit of the new learning and religious reform.

(*b*) *John Colet, Erasmus, and Thomas More.*

John Colet was son of a lord mayor of London, and

likely to succeed to his father's fortune. His earnest religious spirit made him wish to enter the Church. In Italy he studied the writings of Pico and Ficino and Plato, and above all the Bible, and returned to Oxford full of zeal for the new learning and for reform.

He at once began to lecture at Oxford on St. Paul's Epistles, trying to find out what they meant in the same common sense way that men would use to understand letters written by a living man to his friends; not asking what the learned schoolmen had decided that they meant, but giving the schoolmen the go by (quoting Plato and Pico and Ficino more often than them), and so giving the Epistles a life-like power, interest, and freshness quite new to his hearers. By so doing he hoped to set men's minds free from the scholastic system, to make them inquire into facts for themselves, and drink in at first hand the teachings of the Apostle. *Lectures on St. Paul's Epistles at Oxford.*

For generations men had become monks and clergy-men without even reading the New Testament. Colet found theological students poring over the books of the schoolmen. His lectures were the beginning of a work which went on till it quite revolutionized the theological teaching of the University. For-ty years after, people found the books of the schoolmen set aside as useless, and their torn leaves strung up by the corner as waste paper. *Attacks the schoolmen.*

Colet had seen in Italy how much the ecclesiastical as well as the scholastic system needed reform; and so in his lectures at Oxford he zealously urged the necessity of a reform in the morals of the clergy. He urged that it was ecclesiastical scandals and the wicked worldly living of the clergy, the way they mixed themselves up with poli- *He urges also the need of ecclesi-astical re-form.*

tics, and strove after power and money and pleasure,
which set men against the Church. 'Whereas,' he said,
'if the clergy lived in the love of God and their neigh-
'bours, how soon would then true piety, religion, charity,
'goodness towards men, simplicity, patience, tolerance
'of evil, conquer evil with good! How would it stir up
'the minds of men everywhere to think well of the
'Church of Christ.'

He had seen how wicked the Popes and cardinals of
Rome were ; and so now, at Oxford, he burst out into
hot words, written, as he said, 'with grief and tears,'
against ecclesiastical wickedness in high places. He
spoke of the Popes as 'wickedly distilling poison, to the
'destruction of the Church.' Unless there could be a
reform of the clergy, from the Pope at the head down to
the monks and the clergymen, he saw no chance of
saving the Church. 'Oh, Jesu Christ, wash for us not
'our feet only, but also our hands and our *head!* Other-
'wise our disordered Church cannot be far from death."

A man so earnest was sure to make disciples. Students burdened by scholastic arguments came to him,
He attracts   and gladly accepted his advice to 'keep to
disciples   the Bible and the Apostles' Creed, letting
divines, if they like, dispute about the rest.' They followed him from his lectures to his chambers, and im-
bibed his love for St. Paul ; and along with the new
learning, he stirred up in them that real religion which
consists in the love of God and one's neighbour, and
gives men a new power and ruling motive in life.

Two men especially so came within his influence as to
join themselves with him in fellow-work ; and it was by
and fellow-   their means that it became, in a way in
workers.   which Colet alone never could have made
it, a power all over Europe.

One of them was *Thomas* (afterwards Sir Thomas, and Lord Chancellor) *More*, a young man, ten years Colet's junior, but so earnest, so full of wit and genius, and withal so good-natured and fascinating, that those who knew him fell in love with him. He had caught at Oxford the love of the new learning which Grocyn and Linacre had brought from Italy; and, as we shall see by-and-by, became a hearty fellow-worker with Colet. Rising by his talents to posts of high influence in the state, he became one of the most prominent figures in English history during this era. *Thomas More.*

The other fellow-worker was the afterwards famous *Erasmus.* He was an orphan, and poor. Thrust, when a youth, into a monastery by dishonest guardians, who had tried to force him to become a monk in order to get his little stock of money, he rebelled when he came of age, left the monastery, and, in spite of poverty, earning his living by giving lessons to private pupils, worked his way up to such learning as the University of Paris could give. Wanting to master Greek, and too poor to go to Italy, he came, at the invitation of an English nobleman, to learn it at Oxford. He was just turned thirty (the same age as Colet), but already hard study, bad lodging, and the harassing life of a poor student, driven about and ill-used as he had been, had ruined his health. His mental energy rose, however, above bodily weakness, and he came to Oxford, eager for work, and perhaps for fame. He found the little circle of Oxford students zealous for the new learning and those Greek studies on which his own mind was bent. He became known at once to Colet, Grocyn, and Linacre, and fell in love with More. His own words will best describe what he thought of them. *Erasmus.* *Early life of Erasmus.* *He comes to Oxford.* *Makes friends with Colet and Thomas More.*

G

'When' (he wrote in a letter) 'I listen to my friend
'*Colet*, it seems to me like listening to Plato himself. In
'*Grocyn*, who does not admire the wide range of his know-
'ledge? What could be more searching, deep, and re-
'fined than the judgment of *Linacre?* Whenever did
'nature mould a character more gentle, endearing, and
'happy than *Thomas More's?*

During the time he spent at Oxford, he had many
talks and discussions with Colet. He had come to Ox
ford full of the spirit of the revival of learning, but not

Comes under
Colet's influ-
ence.

yet hating the scholastic system as Colet did,
nor ready at once to take to Colet's views on
the need of reform. He had not yet got the
religious earnestness which made Colet what he was.
But Colet's fervour was infectious; and before Erasmus
left Oxford, he saw clearly what a great work Colet had
begun.

Colet urged him to stay at Oxford, and at once to join
him in his work; but Erasmus said he was not ready—
he must first go to Italy to study Greek, as others had
done. But, he said, 'When I feel that I have the needful firmness and strength, I will join you.' How effectually he did aid him afterwards we shall presently see.

(c) *The Oxford students are scattered till the accession of Henry VIII.* (1500–1509).

During the remainder of the reign of Henry VII.

The three
friends scat-
tered.

(nine years or thereabouts), the little band
of Oxford students was scattered.

Erasmus left England in 1500 for France,
on his way for Italy; but being robbed of his money by
the custom-house officers at Dover, he was obliged by
poverty to stay in France instead of going to Italy.

Colet went on with his work at Oxford as earnestly as

ever, till he was made Dean of St. Paul's, and removed to London.

More worked his way up to the bar in London, became popular in the City, and very early in life went into Parliament.

The last years of Henry VII. were marked by the discontent occasioned by the king's avarice. His two ministers, Empson and Dudley tried all kinds of schemes to exact money from the people without breaking the laws.

Exactions of Empson and Dudley.

'These two ravening wolves' (wrote Hall the chronicler, who lived near enough to the time to feel some of the exasperation he described) 'had such a guard of false 'perjured persons appertaining to them, which were by 'their commandment empanelled on every quest, that the 'king was sure to win, whoever lost. Learned men in the 'law, when they were required of their advice, would say, '"To agree is the best counsel I can give you." By this 'undue means these covetous persons filled the king's 'coffers and enriched themselves. At this unreasonable 'and extortionate doing noblemen grudged, mean men 'kicked, poor men lamented; preachers openly, at Paul's 'Cross and other places, exclaimed, rebuked, and de-'tested; but yet they would never amend.'

The robbing of Erasmus at the Dover custom-house was an instance of one of these legal robberies. Thomas More also suffered from the royal avarice. He was bold enough to speak and vote in Parliament against a subsidy which he thought was more than the king ought to claim. Whereupon his father was fined on some legal but unjust excuse, and he himself had to flee into retirement. He thought of going into a cloister, and becoming a monk; but, under the influence of Colet, who about that time

More offends Henry VII.

was made Dean of St. Paul's, and came to live in Lon-

The circle
of Oxford
students
formed again
in London. don, he married, and waited for better days. When Erasmus came to England again in 1505, he found Colet, More, Grocyn, Lin-acre, and Lilly (another Oxford student who had been to Italy), all living in London. They found him the necessary means for his journey to Italy, and again he left them, promising to return, and hoping then to join them in fellow-work.

In 1509, while Erasmus was in Italy, Henry VII. died.

(*d*) On the accession of Henry VIII. they commence their fellow-work (1509).

The accession of Henry VIII. seemed to the Oxford students like the beginning of an Augustan age. The

Hopes on the
accession of
Henry VIII. other sovereigns of Europe, Maximilian of Germany, Louis XII. of France, and Ferdi-nand of Spain, were old men, and, owing to their constant wars, poor. Henry VIII. was young and, thanks to his father's peaceful foreign policy and unjust exactions, rich. He was, as most young princes are, popular; every one hoped good things from him. The imprisonment and execution of Empson and Dudley re-lieved the people from fear of further exactions. He was handsome, fond of athletic sports, and, in the early years of his reign, it must be admitted, generous and open-handed. A musician, a scholar, and (however fond of pleasure) neglecting neither study nor business, of great energy having his eye everywhere and keeping the reins of government well in his hands, he seemed likely to make a great and popular king.

By the little band of Oxford students his accession was hailed with the highest hopes. He was personally known to some of them, and known to be a friend of the

'new learning.' Colet (already Dean of The Oxford
St. Paul's) was soon made court preacher. students in Court favour.
Thomas More, to the delight of the citizens
of London, was made under-sheriff, and a few years
afterwards, such was the fondness of the king for him,
that, much against his will, he was drawn into the court.
Even the foreign scholar Erasmus was at once recalled
from Rome and settled at Cambridge as Greek professor. There seemed now to be an open door for Revival
and Reform, and all in the sunshine of the young king's
favour.

(e) *Erasmus writes his ' Praise of Folly'* (1511).

Erasmus, having been to Italy, was now ready to join
Colet heartily in fellow-work. On his way from Italy on
horseback, he planned in his mind, and on his arrival
in London, before going to Cambridge, he wrote in
More's house, his 'Praise of Folly,' a satire in Latin on
the follies of the age, which made his name famous
among the scholars of Europe.

He dressed up Folly in her cap and bells, and made
her deliver an oration to her fellow-fools.

Prominent amongst the fellow-fools were the scholastic
theologians whom Colet had taught him to dislike.
'Folly' described them as men who were so Satire on the
proud that they could define everything, who scholastic theologians.
knew all about things of which St. Paul was
ignorant, could talk of science as though they had been
consulted when the world was made, could give you the
dimensions of heaven as though they had been there and
measured it with plumb and line—men who professed
universal knowledge, and yet had not time to read the
Gospels or Epistles of St. Paul.

Monks were described as shut out of the kingdom of

Monks.

heaven in spite of their cowls and their ha-
bits, while wagoners and husbandmen were
admitted.

'Folly' claimed also among her votaries *Popes* who
(as Julius II. was then doing), instead of 'leaving all,'

Popes.

like St. Peter, try to add to St. Peter's patri-
mony, as they called it, fresh possessions
by war, and turn law, religion, peace, and all human affairs upside down.

This bold satire did much to open the eyes of men all
over Europe to the need of reform, turned the ridicule
of the world upon the scholastic theologians and monks,
and as a natural consequence, raised against Erasmus
the hatred of those whose follies he had so keenly satirized.

This little book written, he went to Cambridge to labour
as Greek professor, and also at another great work of
which we shall have to say more by-and-by—his edition
of the New Testament.

(*f*) *Colet founds St. Paul's School.*

Colet, meanwhile, went on preaching from his pulpit
at St. Paul's. On his father's death he came into posses-

Colet founds a
school of the
new learning.

sion of his fortune, and nobly devoted it to
the foundation of a public school by the
cathedral—in which boys, instead of being
crammed in the scholastic learning, were to be trained
in the new learning, and instead of being taught the bad
Latin of the monks, were to be taught the pure Latin and
Greek which the Oxford students had imported from
Italy; and lastly, instead of being flogged and driven,
were to be attracted and gently led into the paths of
learning.

Lilly was appointed schoolmaster. Erasmus and Linacre were set to work to write school-books, and finding that no one else seemed able to write a Latin Grammar simple and easy enough for beginners, Colet wrote one himself. In his preface he said he had aimed, for the love and zeal he had for his new school, at making his little book on the eight parts of speech as easy as he could, 'judging that nothing may be too soft nor too familiar for little children, specially learning a tongue unto them all strange,' and asking them to 'lift up their little white hands' for him, in return for his prayers for them. Compare with these gentle words the practice of the common run of schoolmasters described by Erasmus, who, too ignorant to teach their scholars properly, had to make up for it by flogging and scolding, defending their cruelty by the theory that it was the schoolmaster's business to subdue the spirits of his boys!

When it was noised abroad that in this new school of the Dean's, classical Latin and Greek were to be taught instead of the bad Latin of the monks, and that under the shadow of St. Paul's cathedral there was thus to be a school of the new learning, men of the old school of thought began to take alarm. More had
jokingly told Colet that it would be so, for
he said the school was like the wooden
horse filled with armed Greeks for the destruction of barbarian Troy; and so the men of the old school regarded it. In spite of the inscription on the building—

Excites the malice of men of the old school.

> Schola Catechizationis Puerorum in Christi
> Opt. Max. fide et bonis literis,

—one bishop denounced it openly as a 'temple of idolatry,' and the Bishop of London began to contrive how to get Colet convicted of heresy, and so a stop put to his work.

About this time there was a convocation, and the Archbishop of Canterbury gave Colet the duty of preach-
Colet's sermon ing to the assembled bishops and clergy the
on ecclesiasti- opening sermon. He took the opportunity
cal reform. of urging, in the strongest and most earnest manner, the necessity of a radical reform in the morals of the clergy. He told them to their face boldly that the wicked worldly life of some of the bishops and clergy was far worse heresy than that of poor Lollards, twenty-three of whom the Bishop of London had just been compelling to abjure, and two of whom he had burned in Smithfield a few months before.

No wonder the Bishop's anger was kindled still more against Colet. He and two other bishops of the old
Escapes from a school joined in laying a charge of heresy
charge of against him before the Archbishop, but the
heresy. latter wisely would not listen to the charge.

So the cause of the new learning prospered during the early years of Henry VIII.

(g) *The Continental Wars of Henry VIII. 1511-1512.*

If we look back to the section on Italy, and the summary there given of Papal and Continental politics, we shall see that it was in 1511 and 1512 that Pope Julius
The Holy Al- II. was bent upon uniting Spain, England,
liance against and Germany in a war against France. Louis
France. XII. had got possession of Milan, and was becoming dangerous. The Pope's object was to drive Louis out of Italy. Ferdinand of Spain wanted not only to get rid of the rivalship of France in Italy, but also to annex the province of Navarre to Spain. Henry VIII.

was tempted to revive the claims of England on the Duchy of Guienne, which since the close of the Hundred Years' War had been annexed to the French Crown. The Emperor Maximilian was always anxious to enlarge his borders at the expense of France. So these princes formed what was called 'the Holy Alliance,' with the

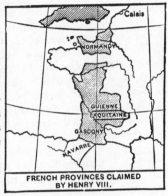

FRENCH PROVINCES CLAIMED
BY HENRY VIII.

Pope at their head, against France, and in 1511 the holy war began. The campaign of that year ended in the crafty Ferdinand getting and keeping Navarre, while Henry the Eighth's invasion of Guienne miserably failed. His troops mutinied, and returned to England in utter disorder.

Henry VIII.'s first campaign.

In the spring of 1513 preparations were being made for another campaign on a greater scale. It was in these preparations that his great minister Wolsey's great talents came into play. Henry VIII. had set his heart on a brilliant invasion of France in order to wipe out the dishonour of the last campaign. He watched the equipment of his fleet, and ordered Admiral Howard to tell him 'how every ship did sail.'

Wolsey.

Just as everything was ready Julius II. died, and the Cardinal de' Medici, Linacre's fellow-student, whose acquaintance Erasmus had made in Italy, was elected Pope under the title of Leo X. The new Pope cared for literature and art and

Julius II. succeeded by Leo X.

building St. Peter's at Rome more than for war, and expressed his anxiety to bring about a peace. But Henry
VIII. had set his heart upon a glorious war,
and in spite of the death of the head of the
Holy Alliance, and in spite also of his
father-in-law Ferdinand's hanging back at the last moment, he was determined to go on. Admiral Howard in
his first engagement with the French, lost his life in a
brilliant exploit, and his crew, disheartened, returned to
Plymouth. But still Henry VIII. set sail with the rest
of the ships for Calais, with 'such a fleet as Neptune
never saw before,' and from Calais he
marched his army a few leagues beyond the
French frontier, took some towns of small
importance, and turned the French army to flight at the
Battle of the Spurs.

But Henry persists in invading France.

Gains the Battle of the Spurs

He did little harm to France or good to England, but
got some sort of a victory, and so gratified his vanity.
There were of course great rejoicings, tournaments, and pageants, but just in the midst
of them came the news that the Scotch,
always troublesome neighbours in those days, before the
union of the two kingdoms, had, incited by France, taken
the opportunity of Henry VIII.'s absence in France to
invade England, but that through the zeal and energy
of Queen Catherine they had been defeated, and the
King of Scots himself slain, with a host of
the Scotch nobility, at the Battle of Flodden.
Whereupon Henry VIII., finding nothing better to do,
amid great show of rejoicing returned to England, bent
upon preparing for another invasion by-and-by.

Scotch invasion of England.

Battle of Flodden.

But his father-in-law, Ferdinand, had served him so
badly in these two campaigns—leaving him to bear the
brunt of them, while he contented himself with taking

and keeping Navarre—that the end of it was a strange shuffling of the cards. Henry VIII. made peace with Louis XII., and England and France combined to wrest back again from Spain that very province of Navarre which Henry VIII. had helped Ferdinand to wrest from France only a few years before.

Henry VIII. now joins France against Spain.

In January 1515 this unholy alliance was broken by Louis XII.'s death. He was succeeded by Francis I.., who, eager, like his young rival, Henry VIII., to win his spurs in a European war, at once declared his intention that the ' monarchy of Christendom should rest under the banner of France, as it was wont to do!' A few months after, he started on the Italian campaign, in which, after defeating the Swiss soldiers at the battle of Marignano, he recovered the Duchy of Milan.

Louis XII. succeeded by Francis I.

Francis I. invades Italy, and recovers Milan.

Again both Ferdinand and Henry VIII. were made friends by their common jealousy of France. It would never do to let France become the first power in Europe.

Again England and Spain combine against France.

So during these years, instead of an Augustan age of peace, reform, and progress in the new learning and civilization, through the jealousy and lust of military glory of her kings, stirred up by the late warlike Pope and his Holy Alliance, Europe was harried with these barbarous wars!

These wars of kings against the interests Europe.

We have seen, in the chapter on France, how her national wars tended to increase the power of the Crown, and how the fact that the Crown was absolute and backed by its standing army, while it tended to keep France a united kingdom on the map, injured the nation. So it was

They tended to make kings absolute.

The example of France.

also in measure—happily only in measure—in England. These wars tended to make the king absolute. To carry them on, not only were all the hoarded treasures of Henry VII. dispersed, but fresh taxes were needed; and when all the taxes were spent that could be got legally out of votes of Parliament, Wolsey was driven to get more money by illegal means.

Narrow escape of England.

Had the war-fever gone on a little longer—just so long as to establish the precedent of the king's levying taxes without consent of Parliament—then England might well have lost her free constitution, just as France had already done. But, happily, this was not so to be.

In the meantime, let us see how the Oxford Reformers acted in this crisis of European affairs, how they used all their influence to set the public opinion of the educated world against this evil policy of European princes.

Colet preaches against the wars.

Colet preached against the wars to the people from his pulpit at St. Paul's, and to the king from the pulpit of the royal chapel; and his enemies tried to get him into trouble with the king for doing so. But Henry VIII., wild as he was for military glory, was generous enough to respect the sincerity and boldness of the dean; and though not wise enough to follow his advice, refused to stop his preaching. Erasmus made known to his learned friends all over Europe this bold conduct of Colet and his hatred of war. He also, in his

Erasmus against them too,

letters to the Pope, princes, cardinals, bishops, and influential men everywhere, protested against the false international policy which sacrificed the good of the people to the ambition of kings.

and also More.

More also made no secret to the king that he was opposed to his conquering France, and that he hated the wars.

(*h*) *The kind of Reform aimed at by the Oxford Reformers.*

It so happened that just at this time Erasmus was invited to the court of Prince Charles of the Netherlands (afterwards the Emperor Charles V.), and that More was also being drawn by Henry VIII. into his royal service. They both at length yielded. Erasmus became a privy councillor of Prince Charles, on condition that it should not interfere with his literary work. More became a courtier of Henry VIII. when peace was made with France, on condition that in all things he should 'first look to God, and after Him to the king.'

Erasmus made a councillor of Prince Charles.

More drawn into Henry VIII.'s service.

Both Erasmus and More, in thus entering royal service, published pamphlets or books containing a statement of their views on politics. Erasmus called his 'The Christian Prince;' More called his a 'Description of the Commonwealth of Utopia.'

Erasmus, in his 'Christian Prince,' urged that the *Golden Rule* ought to guide the actions of princes—that they should never enter upon a war that could possibly be avoided, that the good of their people should be their sole object, that it was the people's choice which gave a king his title to his throne, that a constitutional monarchy is much better than an absolute one, that kings should aim at taxing their people as little as possible; that the necessaries of life, things in common use among the lowest classes, ought not to be taxed, but luxuries of the rich, and so on: the key-note of the whole being that the object of nations and governments is the common weal of the whole people.

The 'Christian Prince' of Erasmus.

In the meanwhile, More, in his 'Utopia,' or description of the manners and customs of an ideal common-

More's
'Utopia.'

wealth ('Utopia' meaning 'nowhere'), urged
just the same points. The Utopians
elected their own king, as well as his council or parliament. They would not let him rule over another
country as well: they said he had enough to do to
govern their own island. The Utopians hated war as
the worst of evils; the Utopians aimed not at making
the king and a few nobles rich, but the whole people.
All property belonged to the nation, and so all the people were well off. Nor was education confined to one
class; in Utopia everyone was taught to read and write.
All magistrates and priests were elected by the people.
Every family had a vote, and the votes were taken by
ballot. Thus the key-note of More's 'Utopia' was, like
the 'Christian Prince' of Erasmus, that governments and
nations exist for the common weal of the whole people.

If we turn back to the description already given of
the two points which mark the spirit of modern civiliza-

They
entered
thoroughly
into the
spirit of
modern
civilization.

tion, and judge these sentiments of Erasmus and More from that point of view, we
cannot fail to see how thoroughly they entered into the spirit of the new era, and how
correct and far-reaching were the reforms
which they urged upon the public opinion of Europe.

We must not leave the Oxford Reformers without
trying to get a clear idea of the kind of religious reform
which they urged.

We have seen that Colet's object was to set the minds

The character
of their
religious
reform.

of men free from the bonds of the scholastic
system, by leading men back from the
schoolmen to the teaching of Christ and
His Apostles in the New Testament.

Erasmus had been all this while labouring hard in fellow-work with him. He had for years been working at, and now, in 1516, published at the printing-press at Basle, a book which did more to prepare the way for the religious reformation than any other book published during this era. This was his edition of the New Testament, containing,

in two columns side by side, the original Greek and a new Latin translation of his own. He thus realized a great object, which Colet had long had in view, viz., not only to draw men away from scholastic theology, but to place before them, in all the freshness of the original language and a new translation, the 'living picture' of Christ and His Apostles contained in the New Testament. By so doing he laid a firm foundation for another great religious reform, viz., the translation of the New Testament into what was called 'the vulgar tongue' of each country, thus bringing it within reach of the people as well as of the clergy.

'I wish' (Erasmus said in his preface to his New Testament) 'that even the weakest woman should read 'the Gospels—should read the Epistles of Paul; and I 'wish that they were translated into all languages, so 'that they might be read and understood not only 'by Scots and Irishmen, but also by Turks and Sara-'cens. I long that the husbandman should sing por-'tions of them to himself as he follows the plough, 'that the weaver should hum them to the tune of his 'shuttle, that the traveller should beguile with their 'stories the tedium of his journey.'

Of course this great work of Erasmus excited the oppo-sition and hatred of the men of the old school, and espe-cially of the monks and scholastic divines, to whom the old Vulgate version was sacred, and Greek a heretical

tongue. But the New Testament went through several
large editions, and when, a few years after, the learned
men of the Sorbonne at Paris complained of what they
called its heresies, Erasmus was able to reply triumphantly, 'You are too late in your objections. You
should have spoken sooner. It is now scattered over
Europe by thousands of copies!'

One other point we have to fix in our minds—the
attitude of the Oxford Reformers to the ecclesiastical

The kind of
ecclesiasti-
cal reform
urged by the
Oxford Re-
formers.

system. We have seen that their notion of
religion was that it was a thing of the heart
—the love of God and man. They believed
that it was intended to bind men together
in a common brotherhood, not to divide them

into sects. They complained how rival orders of monks
and schools of theology hated one another. Christians
might differ about doctrines, but they ought to agree in

They aimed
at a broad
and tolerant
Church.

the worship of God and in their love of one
another. Hence More in his Utopia had
described the Utopians as giving full tolera-

tion to all varieties of doctrines and differences of creeds;
and pictured all worshipping together in one united and
simple mode of worship, expressly so arranged as to hurt
the feelings of no sect among them, so that they all might
join in it as an expression of their common brotherhood
in the sight of God.

It is clear that, holding these views, they were likely
to urge, as they did earnestly urge, the reform of the
ecclesiastical system, but that if at any time a great
dissension were to arise in the Church, they would urge
that the Church should be reformed and widened so as

And were
likely to op-
pose schism.

to give offence to neither party, and include
both within it, and would oppose with all
their might anything which should break up

its unity and cause a schism. Whether right or wrong, this would be the course which their own deep convic-tions would be likely to lead them to take, and this, we shall see, was the line the survivors of them did take when the Protestant struggle came on. We say 'the survivors,' because Colet did not live to work much longer. Even now, driven into retirement by the perse-cution of the old Bishop of London, he could do little but work at his school. And he died in 1519.

To the beginning of the Protestant movement we must now turn our attention.

CHAPTER III.

THE WITTENBERG REFORMERS.

(a) *Martin Luther becomes a Reformer.*

MARTIN LUTHER was born in 1483, and so was 15 years younger than Erasmus and Colet, and three years younger even than their young friend More.

Born 1483.

His great-grandfather and grandfather were Saxon peasants, but his father being a younger son had left home and become a miner or slate-cutter at Mansfield in Thuringia. Both his parents were rough and hot-tempered, but true and honest at heart. Though working hard for a living, they sent their sons to school, and wishing Mar-tin to become a lawyer, they found means to send him to the university of Erfurt. There he took his degree of M. A.

Sent to school, and to uni-versity.

In 1505, in fulfilment some say of a vow made in a dreadful thunderstorm, when he thought his end was

H

Becomes a
monk.
near, Luther, contrary to his father's wishes, left his law studies and entered the Augustine monastery at Erfurt. He inherited the superstitious nature of the German peasantry. He traced every harm that came to him through passion and temptation all alike to the Devil. His conscience was often troubled. His fasts and penances did not give him peace. He passed through great mental struggles, sometimes shut himself up in his cell for days, and once was found senseless on the floor. At length he found peace of mind in the doctrine of 'justification by faith,' *i. e.*, that forgiveness of sins, instead of being got by fasts and penances and ceremonies, is given freely to those who have faith in Christ. This doctrine he learned partly from the pious vicar-general cf the monastery, partly from the works of St. Augustine, and under their guidance from a study of the Bible. From this time he accepted also other parts of the theology of St. Augustine, and especially those which, because they

Adopts the
theology of St.
Augustine.

were afterwards adopted by *Calvin*, are now called 'Calvinistic,' such as that all things are fated to happen according to the divine will, that man has therefore no free will, and that only an elect number, predestinated to receive the gift of faith, are saved.

It is well to mark here that these Augustinian doctrines were, in fact, a part of that scholastic theology from which the Oxford Reformers were trying to set men free. In not accepting them they differed from Luther. But they and Luther had one thing in common. They alike held that religion did not consist in ceremonies, but was a thing of the heart; that true worship must be in spirit and in truth.

And in this differed from the
Oxford Reformers.

In 1508 Luther was removed from Erfurt to the Augustinian monastery at Wittenberg, and soon after made preacher there at the University recently founded by the Elector of Saxony.

Luther removes to Wittenberg.

In 1510 he was sent on an errand for his monastery to Rome. There he found wicked priests performing masses in the churches, ignorant worshippers buying forgiveness of sins from the priests, and doing at their bidding all kinds of penances; and he came back zealous, like Colet, for reform, and with the words 'the just shall live by faith' more than ever ringing in his ears.

Visits Rome.

He had been preaching and teaching the theology of St. Augustine at Wittenberg several years with great earnestness, when in 1516 he read the new edition of the New Testament by Erasmus. The works of Erasmus had an honourable place on the shelves of the Elector of Saxony's library, and his New Testament was the common talk of learned men at the universities, even at this youngest of them all —Wittenberg. Luther eagerly turned over its pages, rejoicing in the new light it shed on old familiar passages; but what a disappointment it was to him as by degrees he discovered that there was a great difference between Erasmus and himself—that Erasmus did not accept those Augustinian doctrines on which his own faith was built! He knew that Erasmus was doing a great work towards the needed reform, and this made it all the more painful to find that in these points they differed. He was 'moved' by it, but, he wrote to a friend, 'I keep it to myself, lest I should play into the hands of his enemies. May God give him understanding in his own good time!'

Reads the New Testament of Erasmus.

Finds out the difference in their theology.

This is a fact that in justice to both should never be forgotten. Luther was conscious of it from the first, and it had this future significance, that if Protestantism (as it afterwards did) should follow Luther and adopt the Augustinian theology, Erasmus and the Oxford Reformers never could become Protestants. Luther might wisely try to keep it secret, but if matters of doctrine should ever come to the front, the breach between them was sure to come out.

(*b*) *The Sale of Indulgences* (1517).

While Luther was preaching Augustinian doctrines at Wittenberg, and Erasmus was hard at work at a second edition of his New Testament, pressing More's ' Utopia' and his own ' Christian Prince' on the notice of princes and their courtiers, expressing to his friends at Rome his hopes that under Leo X. Rome might become the centre of peace and religion, Europe was all at once brought by the scandalous conduct of Princes and the Pope to the brink of revolution.

Leo X. wanted money to help his nephew in a little war he had on hand. To get this money he offered to grant indulgences or pardons at a certain price, to those who would contribute money to the building of St. Peter's at Rome. The people were still ignorant enough to believe in the Pope's power to grant pardons for sins, and there was no doubt they would buy them, and so gold would flow into the coffers of Rome. There was one obstacle. Princes were growing jealous of their subjects' money being drawn towards Rome. But Leo X. got over this obstacle by giving them a share in the spoil. He offered Henry VIII. one-fourth of what came from England, but Henry VIII. haggled and bargained to get a third ! Kings had made themselves poor by their wars, and a share in the papal

Leo X.'s schemes to get money by indulgence.

Offers princes a share in the spoil.

spoils on their own subjects was a greater temptation than they could resist.

Erasmus in his ' Praise of Folly ' had described indul-gences as 'the crime of false pardons,' and now in every letter and book he wrote he bitterly complained of the Pope and Princes for resorting to them again.

Erasmus writes bitterly against it.

He wrote to Colet :—

' I have made up my mind to spend the remainder of my life with you in retirement from a world which is everywhere rotten. Ecclesiastical hypocrites rule in the courts of princes. The Court of Rome clearly has lost all sense of shame ; for what could be more shameless than these continued indulgences ! '

And in a letter to another friend, he said :—

' All sense of shame has vanished from human affairs. I see that the very height of tyranny has been reached. *The Pope and Kings count the people not as men, but as cattle in the market !* '

But though Erasmus numbered among his friends Leo X., Henry VIII., Francis I., and Prince Charles, he found them deaf to his satire, and unwilling to reform abuses which filled their treasuries.

But popes and kings will not listen.

They would not listen to Erasmus. It re-mained to be proved whether they would listen to Lu-ther !

(c) *Luther's Attack on Indulgences* (1517.)

Wittenberg was an old-fashioned town in Saxony, on the Elbe. Its main street was parallel with the broad river, and within its walls, at one end of it, near the Elster gate, lay the University, founded by the good Elector—Frederic of Saxony—of which Luther was a professor ; while at the other end of it was the palace of the Elector and the palace church of All Saints. The great parish church lifted its two towers

Wittenberg.

from the centre of the town, a little back from the main street. This was the town in which Luther had been preaching for years, and towards which Tet-

Tetzel comes near, selling indulgences.

zel, the seller of indulgences, now came, just as he did to other towns, vending his 'false pardons'—granting indulgences for sins to those who could pay for them, and offering to release from purgatory the souls of the dead, if any of their friends would pay for their release. As soon as the money chinked in his money-box, the souls of their dead friends would be let out of purgatory. This was the gospel of Tetzel. It made Luther's blood boil. He knew that what the Pope wanted was people's money, and that the whole thing was a cheat. This his Augustinian theology had taught him ; and he was not a man to hold back when he saw what ought to be done. He did see it. On the day before the festival of All Saints, on which the relics of the' Church were displayed to the crowds of country people who flocked into the town, Luther passed down the long street with a copy of ninety-five theses or statements

Luther's theses against indulgences.

against indulgences in his hand, and nailed them upon the door of the palace church ready for the festival on the morrow. Also on All Saints' day he read them to the people in the great parish church.

It would not have mattered much to Tetzel or the Pope that the monk of Wittenberg had nailed up his papers on

He is backed by the Elector of Saxony.

the palace church, had it not been that he was backed by the Elector of Saxony. The Elector was an honest man, and had the good of the German people at heart. Luther's theses laid hold of his mind, and a few days after it is said that he dreamed that he saw the monk writing on the door of his church in letters so large that he could read them eighteen miles off at his palace where he was, and that the pen grew longer and longer, till at last it reached to Rome, touched the Pope's triple crown and made it totter.   He was stretching out his arm to catch it when he awoke!   The Elector of Saxony, whether he dreamed this dream awake or asleep, was at least wide awake enough to refuse permission for Tetzel to enter his dominions.

Then came a year or two of controversy and angry disputes; and just at the right time came *Philip Melanchthon*, from the University of Tubingen, to strengthen the staff of the Elector's new University at Wittenberg—a man deep in Hebrew and Greek, a half-disciple of Erasmus—already pointed out as likely to turn out 'Erasmus II.,' of gentle, sensitive, and affectionate nature, the very opposite of Luther, but yet just what was wanted in another Wittenberg Reformer—to help in argument and width of learning; to be in fact to Luther, partly what Erasmus had been to Colet.   In the weary and hot disputes which now came upon Luther, Melanchthon was always at his elbow, and helped him in his arguments; while the fame of Luther's manly conduct and Melanchthon's learning all helped to draw students to the University from far and near, and so to spread the views of the Wittenberg Reformers more and more widely.

Philip Melanchthon comes to Wittenberg.

(*d*) *The Election of Charles V. to the Empire* (*1519*).

Suddenly, in 1519, the noise of religious disputes was drowned in the still greater noise of political excitement. Maximilian died, and a new Emperor had to be elected.   Prince Charles, who was now King of Spain also, wanted to be Emperor; so did Francis I., though a Frenchman; so

Death of Maximilian. Candidates for the Empire.

did Henry VIII., claiming that, though England was not a subject of the Empire, the English language was a German tongue, while French was not. The princes of the Empire wanted the Elector of Saxony to be Emperor, but he was the one man who cared most for the interests of Germany, and had least selfish ambition.

It was a question which of the three princes could bribe a majority of the seven Electors. Henry VIII. did not risk enough to give himself a chance. It was not

Charles V. elected through the influence of the Elector of Saxony

really likely that, however much they might be bribed, the Electors, who were all German princes, would choose a Frenchman. The Elector of Saxony practically decided the election in favour of Prince Charles.

The following letter of Erasmus, who was a councillor of Prince Charles, will show what manner of man the good Elector was.

'The Duke Frederic of Saxony has written twice to me in reply to my letter. Luther is supported solely by his protection. He says that he has acted thus for the sake rather of the cause than of the person (of Luther). He adds, that he will not lend himself to the oppression of innocence in his dominions by the malice of those who seek their own, and not the things of Christ.' . . . 'When the imperial crown was offered to Frederic of Saxony by all (the Electors), with great magnanimity he refused it, the very day before Charles was elected. And Charles never would have worn the imperial title had it not been declined by Frederic, whose glory in refusing the honour was greater than if he had accepted it. When he was asked who he thought should be elected, he said that no one seemed to him able to bear the weight of so great a name but Charles. In the same noble spirit he firmly refused the 30,000 florins offered him by our people (*i. e.* the agents of Charles). When he was urged that at least he would allow 10,000 florins to be given to his servants, "They may take them" (he said) "if they like, but no one shall remain my servant another day who accepts a single

piece of gold." The next day he took horse and departed, lest
they should continue to bother him. This was related to me as
entirely credible by the Bishop of Liege, who was present at the
Imperial Diet.'

Would that Charles V. had followed throughout his
reign the counsels of the good Elector to whom he owed
his crown! Charles's grandfather, Ferdinand, had died
only a few months before, and he was himself in Spain,

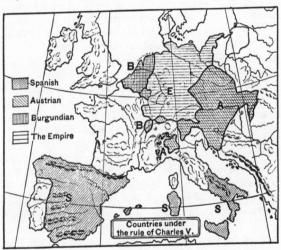

Countries under
the rule of Charles V.

settling the affairs of his new kingdom, when he was
elected. We have now to mark what power had fallen
into the hands of this prince of the House of Hapsburg.
On the map are distinguished the Austrian, Extent of
Burgundian, and Spanish provinces which Charles V.'s
rule.
came under his rule. We must remember,
too, how the ambition of Spain was to increase its Ital-

ian possessions, and that, as head of the 'Holy Roman Empire,' he was also nominally King of Italy!

(e) *Luther's Breach with Rome* (1520).

While these political events had been absorbing attention, the religious disputes between Luther and the papal party had been going on.

Luther finds nimself a Hussite.

They had this singular effect upon Luther: they drove him to see that his Augustinian views were identical with those of Wiclif and Huss. He was astonished, as he described it, to find that 'he was a Hussite without knowing it; that St. Paul and Augustine were Hussites!'

The fact was that Wiclif and Huss, like Luther, had in a great degree got their views from the works of St. Augustine: they had so adopted many of the doctrines which belonged to what we have said is now called the *Calvinistic* theology.

This discovery hastened on his quarrel with the Pope. The Pope and Councils had denounced Wiclif and Huss as heretics; therefore Popes and Councils were not infallible.

Rumoured Papal Bull against Luther.

This was the conclusion to which Luther came. Luther had declared himself a Hussite, therefore the papal party contended he must, like Huss, be a heretic; and the long continuance of the Hussite wars being taken into account he must be a dangerous heretic. So the Pope made up his mind to issue a Papal Bull against Luther.

When rumours of this reached Luther, so far from being fearful, he became defiant. He at once wrote two pamphlets.

The first was addressed ' *To the Nobility of the German nation.*' It was published, in both Latin and German, in

1520, and 4,000 copies were at once sold. If we bear in mind what has already been said in the section 'On the Ecclesiastical System,' the chief points of the pamphlet will be easily understood.

The gist of it was as follows:—

'To his Imperial Majesty and the Christian Nobility of the German nation, Martin Luther wishes grace, &c. The Romanists have raised round themselves walls to protect themselves from reform. One is their doctrine, that there are two separate estates; the one *spiritual*, viz. pope, bishops, priests, and monks; the other *secular*, viz. princes, nobles, artisans, and peasants. And they lay it down that the secular power has no power over the spiritual, but that the spiritual is above the secular; whereas, in truth, *all* Christians are spiritual, and there is no difference between them. The secular power is of God, to punish the wicked and protect the good, and so has rule over the whole body of Christians, without exception, pope, bishops, monks, nuns and all. For St. Paul says, 'Let *every* soul (and I reckon the Pope one) be subject to the higher powers.' [Luther was writing this to the secular princes, and they were likely to listen to this setting up of their authority above that of the clergy. He was writing also to the German nation, and he knew well how to catch their ear too.] 'Why should 300,000 florins be sent every year from Germany to Rome? Why do the Germans let themselves be fleeced by cardinals who get hold of the best preferments and spend the revenues at Rome? Let us not give another farthing to the Pope as subsidies against the Turks; the whole thing is a snare to drain us of more money. Let the secular authorities send no more annates to Rome. Let the power of the Pope be reduced within clear limits. Let there be fewer cardinals, and let them not keep the best things to themselves. Let the national churches be more independent of Rome. Let there be fewer pilgrimages to Italy. Let there be fewer convents. Let priests marry. Let begging be stopped by making each parish take charge of its own poor. Let us inquire into the position of the Bohemians, and if Huss was in the right, let us join with him in resisting Rome.'

And then, at the end, he threw these few words of defi.
ance at the Pope:—

'Enough for this time! I know right well that I have sung in a
high strain. Well, I know another little song about Rome and her
people! Do their ears itch? I will sing it also, and in the highest
notes! Dost thou know well, my dear Rome, what I mean?'

His other pamphlet—his 'other little song about Rome'
—was an attack upon her doctrines. It was entitled

Another pam-
phlet on the
' Babylonish
Captivity of
the Church.' ' *On the Babylonish Captivity of the Church,*'
and in it he repeated his condemnation of
indulgences, denied that the supremacy of
the Pope was of divine right, declared the
Pope a usurper, and the Papacy the kingdom of Baby-
lon; and then, turning to matters of doctrine, boldly reduced the sacraments of the Church, by an appeal to
Scripture, from seven to three—Baptism, Penance, and
the Lord's Supper. He ended this pamphlet in as defiant
a tone as the other. 'He heard' (he said) 'that Bulls
' and other terrible Papistical things were being prepared,
'by which he was to be urged to recant or be declared a
'heretic. Let this little book be taken as a part of his
'recantation, and as an earnest of what was to come!'

While the printing-press was scattering thousands of
copies of these pamphlets all over Germany, in Latin for

The Bull
arrives. the learned, and in German for the common people, the Bull arrived, and the
Elector of Saxony was ordered by the Pope to deliver
up the heretic Luther. The question now was, What
would Luther do with the Bull, and the Elector with
Luther?

(*f*) *The Elector of Saxony consults Erasmus,*
December 6, 1520.

Much at this moment depended on what the good
Elector of Saxony would do. Well was it that the fate

of Luther lay in the hands of so conscientious a prince.
He and his secretary Spalatin were at Cologne, where
Charles V., after his recent coronation, was holding his
court. Melanchthon and Luther were in constant corres-
pondence with Spalatin. Melanchthon wrote that all
their hopes rested with the prince, and urged Spalatin to
do his best to prevent Luther being crushed,—'a man,'
he said, 'who seemed to him almost inspired, and
whom he dared to put not only above any other man
of the age, but even above all the Augustines and
Jeromes of any age!' So enthusiastic a disciple of the
bold Luther had the gentle Melanchthon become!
Spalatin did his best.

Aleander, the Pope's nuncio, and supposed author of
the 'Bull,' was at Cologne, wild against Luther and
doing all he could to get the Emperor to make common
cause with the Pope.   He knew that the Elector of
Saxony stood in the way, and did his best *Aleander,*
to win him over. Erasmus, being one of *the Pope's*
the Emperor's council, also was there, and *nuncio, tries*
Aleander knew that he, too, was against *the Elector*
the crushing of the poor monk, and if he *of Saxony.*
could have bribed him over with a bishopric, or secretly
poisoned him, there is evidence that it would most likely
have been done. The Elector was bent upon doing what
was right and best for Germany and for Christendom,
and anxious to have the advice of the best and the
wisest men upon the course he should take. Erasmus
had written to the Wittenberg Reformers, praising their
zeal, but advising more gentleness. Melanchthon had
sent the letter from Erasmus to the good Elector,
who now wanted to consult Erasmus confidentially himself. Spalatin managed the interview. It was in the
Elector's rooms at the inn of 'The Three Kings' that

they met, the Elector, Erasmus and Spalatin. The Elector asked of Erasmus through Spalatin, in Latin, as they stood over the fire, 'What he really thought of
The Elector asks advice of Erasmus. Luther?' and fixed his eyes eagerly upon him as he waited for an answer. Erasmus said, with a smile, 'Luther has committed two crimes! He has hit the Pope on the crown and the monks on the belly.'

This was exactly the truth. The Elector's dream had come true. Luther's great pen had reached to Rome and touched the Pope's triple crown. Leo X. was a sort of patron of Erasmus, but that did not hinder Erasmus from condemning the Bull. The monks were his old enemies, bitter against the new learning, haters of himself and Colet as well as Luther, because they saw their craft was in danger as men's eyes became more and more opened. Therefore Erasmus could afford to smile a bitter sarcastic smile at the expense of both Pope and monks. Before he left he wrote down on paper a short
The advice of Erasmus. statement of his opinion that the monks' hatred of the new learning was at the bottom of their zeal against Luther, whilst only two universities had condemned him; that Luther's demand to be properly heard was a fair one; and that being a man void of ambition, he was less likely to be a heretic. At all events the views of Luther's opponents were worse than his; all honest men disapproved of the Bull; and clemency was what ought to be expected of the new Emperor.

While thus he spoke in favour of fair dealing with Luther, he at the same time found much fault with Lu-
The Elector follows it. ther's violent way of going to work and his abusive language. The result of the interview was reported to Luther. Melanchthon and he were

well satisfied with the advice given by Erasmus. They
considered that it had great weight in strengthening the
Elector in favour of Luther. At all events the Elector
followed it in two points—he remained firm in defence
of Luther, and at the same time he wrote and recom-
mended to Luther more of that gentleness the want of
which had displeased Erasmus.

(*g*) *Luther burns the Pope's Bull, December* 10, 1520.

Perhaps the advice of the Elector to Luther came just
too late! The meeting with Erasmus at the inn of the
'Three Kings' at Cologne was on December 5. In the
meantime Luther had been making up his mind what to
do, and on the 10th he did it, we may suppose before the
posts from Cologne had reached him.

Excited, and as Melanchthon said, seeming almost
inspired, conscious of right and also of power, Luther
wished all Europe to see that a German monk could dare
to defy the Pope. Had there been a mountain at Wittenberg he would have lit his bonfire on the top, and let
the world, far and near, see the Pope's Bull blaze in its
flames. But there was not even a hill in that   Luther
flat country. So in solemn procession, at   burns the
the head of his fellow-doctors and the stu-   Bull.
dents of the university, he marched through the Elster
gate, and there, outside the city walls, in presence of the
great German river Elbe, he burned the Bull, and as
many Roman law books as he could find. His burning
the Bull against himself was a personal act of defiance.
His burning the Roman law books was a public decla-
ration that the German nation ought not to be subject to
the jurisdiction of Rome. Amid the cheers of the crowd,
Luther returned to his rooms. That a man of hot tem-
per, fastening by his daring act the eyes of all Europe

upon himself, assuming as it were the leadership of a national crusade against the Pope of Rome, should be for
the moment carried away by excitement into extrava-
gance was only natural. Luther was in fact greatly
excited, and on the next day, in his crowded lecture-
room, let himself utter wild words, declaring that those
who did not join in contending against the Pope could
not be saved, and that those who took delight in the
Pope's religion must be lost for ever. He then wrote an
abusive reply to the Bull, hurling all sorts of bad names
against the Pope, and pushing his Augustinian doctrines
to so extreme a point as to amount to fatalism.

Grand as is the figure of Luther on the page of history,
as, in December 1520, he dared to make himself the
mouth-piece of Germany, demanding reform, threatening
revolution if reform could not be had, it must be admitted
Erasmus that he was playing with fire. Was not the
fears revolu-
tion.
train already laid for revolution? Will not
such wild words lead to still wilder acts of
the ignorant peasantry? Sober-minded lookers on, like
Erasmus, feared this. He had feared from the first that
Luther's want of discretion might bring on a 'universal
revolution,' and had therefore urged moderation. Instead
of moderation had come still wilder defiance. 'Now,'
he wrote, 'I see no end of it but the turning upside down
'of the whole world. . . . When I was at Cologne I
'made every effort that Luther might have the glory of
'obedience and the Pope of clemency, and some of the
'sovereigns approved this advice. But lo and behold,
'the burning of the Decretals, the "Babylonish captivi-
'ty;" those propositions of Luther, so much stronger
'than they need be, have made the evil apparently
'incurable.'

CHAPTER IV.

THE CRISIS.—REFORM OR REVOLUTION.—REFORM REFUSED BY THE RULING POWERS.

(*a*) *Ulrich von Hutten and Franz von Sickingen.*

THE fears of Erasmus were well founded. There were wilder spirits in Germany than Luther.

Not far north of Worms, where the first Diet of the Emperor Charles V. was going to meet, was the castle of Ebernburg, where the bold knight *Franz von Sickingen* had gathered round him the chiefs of these wild spirits. Franz himself was a wild lawless knight, living upon private war, hiring out himself and his soldiers to fight out private quarrels, and, like his relative *Goetz von Berlichingen,* popular because of his bravery and rough justice. Goetz and Franz might be said to be in many respects, the Robin Hoods of Germany. The Robin Hoods of Germany side with Luther.

Such a man as Franz was sure to side with Luther though he had already engaged himself and his soldiers for hire to the Emperor Charles V. One of his guests at the castle was *Ulrich von Hutten*, a knight like himself, but there was this difference Ulrich von Hutten. between them. Hutten's pen was his lance. Placed like Erasmus in his youth in a cloister, he too had torn himself from it and taken to a literary life. Not so learned, but with even keener wit than Erasmus, neglect, poverty, and suffering had embittered more his wild warlike spirit. His pen was ever ready to be dipped in gall, and following the example set by Erasmus in his ' Praise of Folly,' he tried to mend the world by satire. His satire upon Rome. He had been to Rome, and in Latin rhyming verses he held up her vices to scorn, He pointed out

I

in these rhymes how German gold flowed into the coffers
of the 'Simon of Rome.' He sneered at the blindness
and weakness of the German nation in letting themselves be the dupes of Rome. When Luther came upon
the scene, Hutten's heart was stirred. He made his re-
solve to rush into the fight against Rome The fears and
tears of his family could not stop him. He was disin-
herited for doing it, but do it he must. Hitherto his
rhymes had been in Latin, and thus only read by the
learned. Henceforth he would write in German for the
Fatherland.

His German
popular
rhymes
against
Rome.

> In Latin hitherto I've written,
> A tongue all did not understand :—
> Now call I on the Fatherland,
> The German nation, in her mother tongue,
> To avenge these things.

'Germany must abandon Rome. Liberty for ever!
The die is cast.' This was the cry of his popular German rhymes.

To Luther he held out the hand of devoted friend-
ship :—

> Servant of God, despair not!
> Could I but give a helping hand,
> Or in these matters counsel thee,
> So would I spare nor goods
> Nor my own blood!

And on the eve of the Diet of Worms he issued his
*'Complaint and exhortation against the extravagant and
unchristian power of the Pope,'* in rhyme, in which he
exposed the tyranny, wealth, worldliness, and cost to
Germany of Rome, and tried to lash up the German people into rebellion against it. Now was the time to free

Demands
freedom from
Rome.

Germany from the Roman yoke. He appealed to the Emperor as the natural leader
of the German nation. It would redound

to his honour. He alone should be the captain.
All free Germans would serve with gladness the sa-
viour of their country. ' Help, worthy king, unfurl the
' standard of the eagle, and we will lift it high. If warn-
' ings will not do, there are steeds and armour, halberts
' and swords, and we will use them!'

There was something pathetic in this cry of the Germans to their Emperor. The very peasants of the
' *Bundschuh*' we saw would have made him their leader,
had he listened to their appeal against their feudal op-
pressors, and now the German nation was beseeching
him to head their rebellion against Rome! These were
but outbursts of a general yearning for unity among the
German people. They felt the necessity of central
power as the only cure for the evils under which they
suffered, and now when the quarrel of Luther and the
Pope had brought ecclesiastical grievances to the top,
the question was whether Charles V., in his first Diet,
would side with the German nation, or sell the German
nation for his own selfish objects to the Pope!

Meanwhile appearances were ugly. Luther wrote to
Spalatin: ' I expect you will return with the stale news
that there is no hope in the court of Charles.' Small chances
Erasmus wrote: ' There is no hope in of reform.
Charles; he is surrounded by Sophists and Papists.'
But Hutten hoped against hope. Such men are san-
guine. If Charles would do his duty to Germany in the
Diet of Worms, all might be well. If not, Hutten was
ready for revolution. Sickingen had soldiers; with the
pen and the sword they would rise in rebellion.

(*b*) *The Diet of Worms meets 28th January, 1521.*

Let us, for a moment, leave these wilder spirits and
try to understand what it was that the more sober-

minded of the German people expected from the Diet of Worms.

Happily there is among English State papers a copy of 'Agenda,' or as it is headed, 'A memory of divers matters to be provided in the present Diet of Worms.'

Agenda' at the Diet of Worms.

The following are the chief heads, and in these we cannot fail to recognize what in former chapters we have found to be the real grievances of the German nation.

(1) To make some ordinance that no man without consent of the Emperor and Electors shall for any personal cause presume to declare war as in times past. On this the cities and towns are determined to stick fast.

To stop private war.

(2) To settle certain disputes between various parties. (There be above thirty bishops at variance with their temporal lords for their jurisdiction.)

To settle disputes.

To provide central power in the Emperor's absence.

(3) The Emperor to provide a vicar and council in his absence. If the Duke of Saxony will not take the charge, there will be great difficulty in finding one who will please the generality, for enmities are so numerous.

(4) To take notice of the books and descriptions made by Friar Martin Luther against the Court of Rome. The which Friar Martin, of the Elector of Saxony and other princes is much favoured.

Martin Luther.

We have here a list of the chief grievances before noticed. (1) The evil of the constant private wars of the nobles, especially to the commerce of the towns. (2) The constant quarrels between the civil and ecclesiastical powers. (3) The want of a central government. (4) The Lutheran complaints against Rome. Only the grievances of the poor peasants find no voice!

Perhaps it was not likely they should.   They had no friends at court.   They had tried to make their voice heard sword in hand, and had not their re-   No hope
bellions been quelled and their standard of   for the
the *Bundschuh* trodden in the dust?   Had   peasantry
not even Joss Fritz been lost sight of for years?   It was not their silent grievances, but the more noisy ones which were to be heard at the Diet.

The Diet was opened by Charles V. on the 28th January, 1521.

The first business was the appointment of a Council of Regency to manage the affairs of the Empire during the Emperor's projected absence in Spain.   Then came the establishment of an imperial chamber, and the granting of an impost or tax to defray the expenses of the government.

These political matters were proceeding, when one day in February on which a tournament was to be held and the Emperor's banner was hoisted   Brief from
ready for the lists, the princes were called   Rome about
together to hear read a brief just arrived   Luther.
from Rome.   This brief exhorted the Emperor to add the force of law to the Pope's Bull against Luther by an imperial edict.   The Emperor had now an opportunity of showing that the unity of the Church was as dear to him as to the Emperors of old.   He wore the sword in vain if he did not use it against heretics, who were far worse than infidels.   So urged the Pope.   The Emperor had already had Luther's books burned in the Nether-lands, and he now produced to the princes an edict commanding the rigorous execution of the Bull in Germany.   He was evidently ready to yield to the wishes of the Pope, but it was needful to consult the Electors.   Some of the Electors were of course not pre-

The Electors hesitate to sanction the edict against Luther. pared to accept the proposal of the Emperor. In order to persuade them, Aleander, the papal nuncio, delivered at another session of the Diet a speech nine hours in length, in which he inveighed against the heresies of Luther, urged that he should be condemned unheard, and declared that 'unless the heresy were stopped, Germany would be reduced to that frightful state of barbarism and desolation which the superstition of Mahomet had brought upon Asia.' The Electors seemed to be swayed by his eloquence. They cared little for Luther's doctrinal heresies, nay, they were willing to sacrifice the heretic if the grievances of the German nation against Rome could but be remedied. But these grievances were too real to be passed over so easily.

The Diet, after further delay, appointed a committee to draw up a list of these grievances. Meanwhile the speech of Aleander had been reported to Hutten, who was staying, as we said, at the castle of Franz von

Hutten adjures the Emperor not to yield to Rome. Sickingen, a few miles from Worms. It stirred his wrath to think of Luther's being condemned unheard. At once, on the spur of the moment, he dipped his pen in gall, and wrote letters of violent invective against the papal nuncio and the bishops assembled at Worms. One of them was addressed to the Emperor, declaring that the hope of Germany had been that he would free her from the Romish yoke and put an end to the papal tyranny, and contrasting with these high hopes 'so great an Emperor, the king of so many peoples, cringing willingly to slavery, without waiting even till he is forced.'

'What!' he exclaimed, 'has Germany so ill deserved of thee that with thee, not fighting for thee, it must go to the ground; lead us into danger! Lead us into battle and fire! Let all nations unite against us, all peoples rush upon us, so that at least we may prove our courage in danger! Don't let us, cringing and unmanly, without battle, lie down like women and become slaves!'

Such was the shrill cry of scorn which the course things were taking at Worms called forth from Hutten.

When the list of grievances was brought in at a future sitting of the Diet, the debate was resumed. The complaints against Rome were so strongly put that they made a deep impression on the Diet. The Electors recovered from the effects of the nuncio's speech. The Prince Electors who sided with Luther urged that 'it ' would be iniquitous to condemn a man without hearing ' him, and that the Emperor's dignity and piety were ' engaged that, should Luther retract his errors, those ' other matters should be recognized on which he had ' written so learnedly and Christianly, and that Germany ' should, by the authority of the Emperor, be freed from ' the burdens and tyrannies of Rome.' They urged also the necessity of granting Luther a safe-conduct, and summoning him to appear before the Diet to defend himself.

The Emperor gave way, and on March 6 the summons and safe-conduct were issued, and an imperial herald sent to bring Luther to Worms. Luther summoned to Worms.

(c) *Luther's journey to Worms (1521).*

The herald arrived at Wittenberg, and on April 2 Luther set out for Worms.

That he went with his mind fully made up not to give way or patch up his quarrel with the Pope was shown by this. He left in the hands of *Lucas Cranach*, the great painter of Wittenberg, a series of wood-cuts prepared by Cranach, with explanations in German at the foot, added by Luther's Antithesis of Christ and Antichrist.

himself, depicting the Antithesis, or Contrast between Christ and the Pope. It was, in his own words, 'a good book for the laity.'

He and Hutten, to widen the circle of their readers, and make their appeals to the Fatherland heard by all classes, had scattered their pamphlets in German all over Germany. Luther now called in the aid of these wood-cuts to make his appeal still more popular and telling on the multitude.

Luther had found himself, to his own surprise, following in the track of the Hussites of Bohemia. He had openly avowed it. Indeed, he seems to have been fond of copying some of their acts, perhaps to mark the identity of his object with theirs. They had commenced with burning the Papal Bull, and so had Luther. It was recorded in the Hussite chronicles that one of the things which roused the people in Bohemia against the Pope was the painting by tow Englishmen on the walls of an inn at Prague of two pictures, one representing Christ entering Jerusalem meek and lowly, on an ass; the other the Pope proudly mounted on horseback, glittering in purple and gold. Luther and Cranach had improved upon this example, and produced a series of wood-cuts with a precisely similar intention.

Christ refusing a crown was contrasted with the Pope in his tiara. Christ in the crown of thorns, being beaten and mocked, was contrasted with the Pope on his throne, in all his magnificence. Christ washing the disciples' feet was contrasted with the Pope holding out his sacred toe to be reverently kissed by his courtiers. Christ healing the sick was contrasted with the Pope watching a tournament. Christ bending under the burden of his Cross was contrasted with the Pope borne in state on men's shoulders. Christ driving the money-changers out of the temple was contrasted with the Pope selling his dispensations, and with piles of money before him. Christ's humble entry into Jerusalem was contrasted with the Pope and his retinue in all their glory, but the road they are travelling is shown in the background of the picture to lead to hell. Finally, the Ascension of Christ is contrasted with the descent of the Pope, in his triple crown and papal robes, headlong under an escort of demons and hobgoblins, into the flames of the bottomless pit.

That he left behind him this 'good book for the laity,' to be published in his absence, was a mark of the defiant spirit in which he went to Worms. But underneath this spirit of defiance, it must never be forgotten, was a deep feeling that he was fighting in the cause of God. 'My dear brother,' he said to Melanchthon, in parting, 'if I do not come back, if my enemies put me to death, you will go on teaching and standing fast in the truth ; if *you* live, *my* death will matter little.'

Amidst the tears of his friends, he stepped into the covered wagon and commenced his journey. Others, too, thought he was going out to his death. Luther sets off for Worms. At one place which he passed there was a priest who kept, hanging up in his study, a portrait of Savonarola. He took down the picture from the wall and held it up in silence before Luther. Luther was moved. 'Stand firm,' said the priest, 'in the truth thou hast proclaimed, and God will as firmly stand by thee.' The journey took him twelve days. His journey. He had to pass through Erfurt, the scene of his mental struggles. He spent a night at the old convent, and the next day, contrary to the terms of his safe-conduct, fearlessly preached in the little church of the convent to crowds of people. Earnest tender words were his that day, setting forth that true religion is a thing of the heart, and not of ceremonies or penances, moving multitudes to tears, and making converts. In the midst of it a portion of the crowded building gave way, and people were terrified by the crash. In his wild imagination he set it down to Satan trying to hinder him. All through his journey he seemed to meet with the Devil at every step. If he was fatigued and ill, it was Satan who brought him low; but, he wrote from Frankfort to Spalatin, 'Christ lives, and we will enter Worms in spite of all the gates of Hell and the powers of the air!'

These things did but prove his sense of the importance of the work in which he was engaged. His wild enthusiasm grew out of what was true heroism. The noise, the worship of the crowd, the danger and excitement, would have turned the head of any mere enthusiast. When men are excited they must needs do strange things; and of course on this journey to Worms strange things were done. At one place a parody on the Litany was produced, like the parodies made by modern revolutionary agents:—'Have mercy upon the Germans. 'From the tyranny of the Roman Pontiff deliver the Ger- 'mans. From the insatiable avarice of the Romans 'deliver the Germans. That Martin Luther, that upright 'pillar of the Christian faith, may soon arrive at Worms, 'we beseech Thee to hear us. That the zealous German 'Knight, Ulrich Hutten, the defender of Martin Luther, 'may persevere in upholding Luther, we beseech Thee to 'hear us,' and so on. Of course, wherever the procession stopped at night the inns were full; there were crowds, Popular   vulgar merry-making, and music. Luther excitement.   himself played upon his flute, and doubtless, as his enemies reported, there was no lack of jollity over the beer. All this was in the very nature of things. The point to mark is this—it did not turn the head of Luther.

When news of the enthusiasm occasioned by Luther's progress to Worms arrived at the city, the papal party became alarmed. Charles V. sent his private confessor with messages of compromise, but Luther refused to listen till he reached Worms. It was well he did, for the safe-conduct was nearly expired, and there was danger of treachery. Luther's friends, too, became alarmed. Even Spalatin was afraid of his life if he entered Worms, and reminded him of the fate of Huss, whose safe-conduct availed him little. Luther's noble reply was, 'Huss was burned, but not the truth with him.' He afterwards told the Elector of Saxony, when recalling to mind his own marvellous courage, 'The 'Devil saw in my heart that even had I known that 'there would be as many devils at Worms as tiles upon 'the house-roofs, still I should joyfully have plunged in 'among them!' Luther's he-
roic firmness.

As he drew near the city, six knights and a troop of horsemen of the princes' retinues went out to meet him; and under their escort, the Emperor's herald leading the way, and a great crowd draggling through the streets beside him, in his covered waggon and monk's gown, Luther entered Worms. He enters
Worms.

(d) *Luther before the Diet.*

The next day, towards evening, he was brought before the Diet. The Emperor presided. Six Electors were present, and a large number of archbishops, bishops, and nobility—about two hundred in all. There was a pile of Luther's books on the table. Luther's first
appearance
before the
Diet.

The official then formally put to Luther two questions:

' Do you acknowledge these books to be yours?' 'Do you retract the heretical doctrines they contain?'

Luther replied, ' I think the books are mine;' and,
He asks for
time to consi-
der his an-
swer. after the titles had been read over, 'Yes, the books are mine.' As to the second question, he said it would be rash for him to reply before he had had time for reflection.

The papal party, who had expected to find Luther raging like a lion, began to think he was going to give way. His deportment had been meek and modest. The
They give
him till the
next day. young Emperor turned to one of his courtiers and said, ' This man will never make a heretic of me.' Luther's request for time was allowed till the next day, and on condition that he gave his reply *vivâ voce*.

He was taken back to his inn. People did not know what to make of it. Some thought he would retract. But, in the din and bustle around him, Luther wrote a letter to one of his friends. ' I write to you from the ' midst of the tumult. . . . I confessed myself the author ' of my books, and said I would reply to-morrow touching ' my recantation. *With Christ's help, I shall never re-* ' *tract one tittle !* '

That night there was excitement and noise in the
Excitement
in Worms. streets; quarrels between opposing parties in the crowd, and soldiers rushing about.

The next day Luther prepared himself. He was heard to pray earnestly, and had his Bible open before him. At four o'clock the herald came to bring him before the Diet. The streets were full of people, and spectators looked down from the tops of the houses as the herald led him through passages and private ways to escape the crowd. It was dark before they reached the hall, and torches were lit. As Luther walked up the hall several noblemen met him with encouraging words, amongst whom was the old General *Frundsberg*, of whom we shall hear more hereafter.

The hall was crowded, and some time was lost before the Princes and Electors were settled in their places.

The official at length—two hours after time—opened the proceedings.

Luther's second appearance before the Diet.

' Martin Luther, yesterday you acknowledged the books published in your name. Do you retract those books or not? . . . Will you defend all your writings or disavow some of them?'

Luther replied, in a speech which seemed to his enemies long and rambling; but according to his own and Spalatin's version of it, the pith of what he said was this :—

' Most serene Emperor! Illustrious Princes, &c.,—At the time fixed for me yesterday evening I am here, as in duty bound, and I pray God that your Imperial Majesty will be pleased to listen, as I hope graciously, to these matters of justice and truth. And should I from inexperience omit to give to any one his proper titles, or offend against the etiquette of courts, I trust you will pardon me, as one not used to them.

Luther's speech.

' I beseech you to consider that my books are not all of the same kind.

'(1) There are some in which I have so treated of faith and morals that even my opponents admit that they are worthy to be read by Christian people. If I were to retract these, what should I do but—I alone, among all men—condemn what friends and foes alike hold to be truth!

'(2) Others of my books are against the papacy and popish proceedings—against those whose doctrine and example have wasted and ruined Christendom, body and soul. This no one can gainsay, for the experience of all men, and the complaints of all, bear witness that through the laws of the Pope and the teaching of men the consciences of the faithful have been vexed and wronged, and the goods and possessions of this great German nation by faithless tyranny devoured and drained—yes, and will without end be devoured again! . . . . Now if I were to retract these, I should do nothing but strengthen this tyranny. To its vast unchristian influence I should not only open the windows but the door also, so that it would rage and spoil more widely and freely than it has ever yet dared to do. Under cover of this my recantation, the yoke of its shameless wickedness would become utterly unbearable to the poor miserable people, and it would be thereby established and confirmed all the more if men could say that this had come about by the power and direction of your Imperial Majesty, and of the whole Roman Empire. Good heavens! what a great cloak of wickedness and tyranny should I be!

' (3) The third kind are those books which I have written against some private persons, as, for instance, against those who have undertaken to defend the Roman tyranny, and to oppose what I thought to be the service of God, against whom I know I have been more vehement than is consistent with the character and position of a Christian. For I do not set myself up as holy. I do not, however, dispute for my own life, but the doctrine of Christ. I cannot retract even these books, but I am ready to listen to anyone who, can show me wherein in these books I have erred.'

Here Luther paused. He had spoken in German with, as he thought, modesty, but with great fervour and determination. The perspiration stood on his brow, he was exhausted with the effort of speaking: but when the Emperor, who hardly understood German, ordered him to repeat what he had said in Latin, after whisper-

Repeats his speech in Latin.

ing to a privy counsellor of the Elector of Saxony, who stood by him, he obeyed, and repeated his words in the language which not only Charles but the papal nuncio could understand.

And now, as they understood more fully what he said, the anger of the papal party was naturally more kindled. When he had done, the orator of the Court, betraying his hostility by his manner, declared that Luther's an·

swer was not a fair one. They were not there to dispute
about things that had long ago been settled by Councils.
He demanded a plain, ungarnished answer. Would he
recant or not?

Luther replied:—

'Well, then, if your Imperial Majesty requires a plain answer,
I will give one without horns or teeth! It is this; that I must be
convinced either by the testimony of the Scriptures
or clear arguments. For I believe things contrary
to the Pope and Councils, because it is as clear as
day that they have often erred and said things inconsistent with
themselves. I am bound by the Scriptures which I have quoted;
my conscience is submissive to the word of God : therefore I may
not, and will not, recant, because to act against conscience is unholy
and unsafe. So help me God! Amen.'

Refuses to recant.

One other attempt was made to get him to yield, but
in vain, and night coming on, the Diet was adjourned
to the following morning, to hear the decision of the
Emperor. The princes retired through the dark streets
to their several inns; Luther to his. Frederic of Saxony
sent for Spalatin and expressed his approval of Luther's
conduct, except that perhaps he had spoken too boldly.

Next morning, the 19th April, the Emperor sent to the
princes a message written by his own hand, in French,
declaring his intention to proceed against
Luther as an avowed heretic, and calling
upon the princes to do the same. An attempt was then made by the papal party to induce the
Emperor to rescind the safe-conduct of Luther. The
precedent of Huss was cited. 'Why should not Luther,
with Huss, be burned, and the Rhine receive the ashes
of the one as it had those of the other? This proposal
met with strong opposition from the princes, and was
negatived.

The Emperor decides against Luther.

But while these discussions were going on in the Diet, murmurs were heard out of doors. The proposal to withdraw the safe-conduct roused the righteous indigna-

Threats of revolution.

tion of men like Hutten to the point almost of frenzy. A placard was found posted on the walls of the Town Hall, stating that 400 knights and 8,000 foot were ready to defend Luther against the Romanists. It had no signature, but underneath were written the ominous words, '*Bundschuh, Bundschuh, Bundschuh.*' Rumours came of murmurs and movements of the people in distant parts of Germany. Franz von Sickingen, a few miles off the city, was said to be prepared to take to the sword, and the rumours of this inspired terror in the minds of the papal party, as it gave some colour of likelihood to the threats of Hutten and the placard.

Under the influence of the fears thus excited, the

The Electors urge delay.

Electors prevailed upon the Emperor to give a few days more for a further attempt to shake Luther's firmness.

All was done that could be done to shake it, but without avail. Luther's mind was made up. Let the Pope and the Emperor do their worst, he would stand by his conscience and the Scriptures. At last, on the 26th of

Luther leaves Worms.

April, he received orders from the Emperor to depart on the following day. Twenty-one days were given him for his return to Wittenberg, and on the morrow, escorted as before by the imperial herald, Luther left the crowded streets of Worms and commenced his journey homewards.

What Luther had done at Worms for Germany,

He left Worms the hero of the German nation. He single-handed had fought the battle of Germany against the Pope. He had hazarded his life for the sake of the

Fatherland. It was this which made Luther's name a household word with the Germans for ages to come. There is no name in the roll of German historic heroes so German, national, and typical as Luther's.

But Luther fought a battle at Worms not only for Germany but Christendom—not only against the Pope, but against all powers, religious or secular, who seek to lay chains upon the human mind and to enthrall the free belief of the people. Against the Emperor as well as the Pope, against all powers that be, he asserted the right of freedom of conscience. *and for Christendom.*

(*a*) *Edict against Luther.*

No sooner had Luther left Worms than the papal nuncio set himself to work to perfect his triumph. Luther had not recanted, therefore the Emperor must issue an edict against him.

The threatenings of Hutten had at first made the papal party nervous. They thought that he and Sickingen had really ready a force of soldiers to make good their threats. Everywhere the feeling of the German nation in favour of Luther and against the Pope was apparent, and nowhere more so than at Worms. They felt themselves on dangerous ground. *Fears of the papal party.*

Luther, a few days before leaving the city, wrote an address to the German princes, containing an account of the proceedings at the Diet. This was soon scattered over Germany by the printers, and, just as the minds of the Germans were thus excited in favour of Luther, the rumour spread from city to city, that in spite of his safe-conduct, Luther was captured and had been cruelly treated. Popular indignation was thus roused ; murmurs rose against the Em- *Rumours of Luther's capture.*

K

peror among the princes as well as the common people.
Again the papal party feared nothing less than a general
riot against the emperor and his ecclesiastical advisers,
headed by Hutten and his friends.

But at length news came that Luther was safe in
friendly hands, having been secretly carried off to the
castle of the Wartburg, in Thuringia, and kept there in
safety by his own friends. As the days went by, the
papal party gathering courage, began to laugh at Hutten's
threats as bluster, and strained every nerve to hasten on
the issue of the imperial edict against Luther.

The Elector of Saxony saw the turn things were taking. He saw that Charles was won over by the Pope.

The Elector
of Saxony
leaves
Worms.

He wrote to his brother that it was not only
' Annas and Càiaphas, but Pilate and Herod
also,' that had combined against Luther,
and not caring to remain where he could do no good, he
left Worms.

In fact Aleander, the papal nuncio, had triumphed.
On May 8 a treaty was signed between Charles V. and

Treaty be-
tween
Charles V.
and the
Pope.

the Pope, in which they mutually promised
to have the same friends and the same
enemies, the Pope agreeing to side with the
Emperor, and to exert all his powers to
drive the French out of Milan and Genoa, and the Emperor, as the price of the Pope's alliance, promising to
employ all his powers against Luther and his party.

Aleander had triumphed, and accordingly prepared an
edict against Luther. It required some cleverness to get

The edict
issued
against Lu-
ther.

the sanction of the Electors. The edict was
produced and read unexpectedly in the Emperor's own apartments to such of the Electors as remained in Worms, and received their hasty
approval without discussion. The next Sunday, as

Charles V. was in church, Aleander brought the official copies, and then and there obtained the imperial signature. He took care to date the edict on May 8, 1521, *i. e.*, on the day when the treaty with the Pope was signed, though it was not really signed till some days after, and in the meantime the Elector of Saxony had left.

The secretary of Charles V., *Valdez*, a friend of Erasmus, writing from Worms on May 13, 1521, to a Spanish correspondent, concludes his letter with these remarkable words:

' Here you have, as some imagine, the end of this tragedy, but I am persuaded it is not the end but the beginning of it. For I perceive the minds of the Germans are greatly exasperated against the Romish See, and they do not seem to attach much importance to the Emperor's edicts; for since their publication, Luther's books are sold with impunity at every step and corner of the streets and market-places. From this you will easily guess what will happen when the Emperor leaves.

Letter from Valdez, the Emperor's secretary.

' This evil might have been cured with the greatest advantage to the Christian Republic, had not the Pontiff refused a general council, had he preferred the public weal to his own private interests. But while he insists that Luther shall be condemned and burned, I see the whole Christian Republic hurried to destruction unless God himself help us. Farewell.'

The secretary of Charles V. naturally laid all the blame on the Pope. He little knew how much his master also was to blame. The Elector of Saxony was not far wrong when he hinted that if the Pope and his nuncios were acting the part of Annas and Caiaphas, Charles V. was acting the part of Pilate and Herod.

Let us try to unravel the entangled skein of political motives which influenced his conduct and his treaty with the Pope.

(ƒ) Political reasons for the decision at Worms.

We have seen how the great continental struggle had long been between France and Spain, and how Italy was the battle-field; how both claimed Naples and Milan; how France had been the first to invade Italy;

Rivalship be-
tween Spain
and France.

how France and Spain at one time agreed to share Naples between them; how France got Milan, and then, after the two had quar-relled over the prey, Spain got Naples; how then they had joined again with the Pope and Germany in the league of Cambray against Venice; and how, lastly, the robbers quarrelling again over the spoil, the Pope united Spain, Germany, and England with himself in a holy league to drive France out of Italy, and so France again lost Milan. Then came the succession of young Francis I. to the throne of France, his boast that he would make France the master of Europe, as she was wont to be, his brilliant campaign of 1515 in which he gained the battle of Marignano against the Swiss, and soon after recovered Milan. Then came the struggle for the Empire, and the beginning of the ascendancy of Spain in Europe by Charles V.'s accession to the German throne.

In the political combinations which followed, it was the fate of Francis to be left out in the cold. Leo X.

Intrigues of
princes.

France the
common
enemy of the
Pope, Spain,
and England.

was anxious to league himself in close alli-ance with Charles V., and by his aid to drive the French out of Italy. Henry VIII. was also exceedingly anxious to form a close alliance with Charles V. His mar-riage with Charles' aunt, Catherine of Arra-gon, was already a link between England and Spain. Henry wanted to bring about another by a contract of marriage between Charles V. and the young Princess (afterwards queen) Mary, although she was already engaged to the Dauphin of France. Charles V., in his turn was equally anxious to form such alliances as would strengthen his position against France. He was jealous of the conquests of Francis I. in Italy, and as Emperor of Germany considered himself entitled to Milan, which Francis had conquered. An alliance, therefore, with the Pope and England against France was most to his purpose, but it did not suit his purpose that Henry VIII. should know it.

All the princes were playing a double game and trying to outwit one another. Henry coquetted with Francis in order to make Charles fall in with his wishes out of jealousy. Charles was coquetting both with France and England, proposing marriage with a French princess while he was negotiating with Henry respecting the Princess Mary, and worst of all, while he really intended to marry the Infanta of Portugal. He cared far more for Spain than he did for Germany, and by this match he hoped to unite some day Portugal and Spain. Henry VIII. devised an interview with Francis. Charles was jealous and came over to England. After this meeting with Charles, Henry embarked for France, and met Francis on what, from the grandeur of the preparations, was called the 'Field of the Cloth of Gold.' Immediately afterwards he again met Charles at Gravelines, and did his best to secure his object with Charles while he kept Francis in the dark. But Charles chose a little longer to play fast and loose.

In the meantime the Pope also was playing a double game. Whether to ally himself with Francis, who was preparing his army for another descent upon Italy, or with Charles V. and Henry VIII. against Francis, he kept an open question, though his preference was for the latter plan, if only he could bring Charles V. to his terms ; the chief of them being that Charles should help him to put down the heretic Luther.

The course which things took at the Diet of Worms was ruled by these political intrigues.

The papal party triumphed. The Emperor, as we have seen, concluded an alliance on May 8 with the Pope against France and against Luther.

The consequence was that Europe was to be given over once more to the ambitions and wars of its rival princes. All chances of reform, for the present, were gone. The Diet of Worms came to an end without having accomplished the work which Germany expected from it. Worst of all, the Emperor, instead of siding with Germany against the Pope, had chosen for his private purposes to side with the Pope against Germany.

Reform refused by the ruling powers from political motives.

It is true a council of regency had been established, with the Elector of Saxony at its head, to manage the affairs of the Empire while the Emperor was busied with quelling a rebellion in Spain, and with his wars in Italy. But no decisive steps had been taken to stop those private wars which were the curse of Germany, and of which the cities so bitterly complained. No decisive steps had been taken to remedy the ecclesiastical grievances of which the princes complained. The grievances of the much enduring peasantry had not even been talked of. And as the worst sign of the times, Luther had been condemned by both Pope and Emperor.

The fears of Erasmus were fulfilled, and his bitter words justified by the result. 'Ecclesiastical hypocrites reign in the courts of princes . . . The Pope and Princes treat the people as cattle in the market.'

The reform, both of the Oxford and of the Wittenberg

Reformers, had been refused by the ruling powers. There was nothing left but revolution.

CHAPTER V.

REVOLUTION.

(a) *The Prophets of Revolution* (*1522*).

THE edict of the Emperor issued at the Diet of Worms was published all over Germany. But the papal party were astonished to find how very little peo- . *Popular feel-ing against the Edict.* ple thought of it. The Germans thought a great deal more of the bold conduct of Lu- ther. So that the end of it was that the edict was treated with very much the same neglect as the Pope's Bull. Luther's books were burned in some places under the eye of the Emperor, Everywhere else they were read all the more.

And another thing happened which the papal party had not foreseen. They had for the moment silenced Luther. He was safe in the castle of the *Luther in the Wartburg.* Wartburg, and silent, too, albeit he was hard at work at what would do more to spread the spirit of reform than anything else, viz. translating the Bible into the mother tongue of the Fatherland.

Meanwhile the absence of Luther from his wonted place at Wittenberg did not take away the firebrand as they thought it would, but put it in the hands *In his absence wilder spirit. take the lead.* of the mob. In Luther's absence wilder spirits came to the top. Monks left the con- vents and went to trades. Under the leadership of Carlstadt, the form of public worship was changed. Ex- cited and half-crazy men, carried away by their zeal, set themselves up as prophets and preached strange doc-trines.

At Zwickau, under the range of the Erzgebirge, south of Wittenberg, near Bohemia, lived a weaver of the name of *Claus Storch.* He and some of his comrades fancied they were inspired. They mistook their own ex-cited imaginations for messages from heaven. They wanted no priests, for they were themselves prophets, no Bible, for they were themselves inspired, and they went about preach-ing violent changes, and exciting the crowds who lis-tened to them to violent deeds.

The prophets of Zwickau.

Driven away from Zwickau by the authorities, some of them came to Wittenberg, where the people were already making great changes under the leadership of Carlstadt. Carlstadt was carried away by their zeal, and so were the people. Riots were raised. People went about smash-ing the images in the churches, and even Melanchthon, in Luther's absence, was half inclined to believe in the prophets, though they preached the uselessness of learn-ing and universities.

These things came to the ear of Luther in his retreat at the Wartburg. He at once saw how all this delusion and madness would injure the cause of the Reformation. At the risk of his life he left his place of concealment. He suddenly ap-peared at Wittenberg in his old pulpit. He entreated his old flock to calm their excitement; and not without avail. After ten months' absence, the familiar sound of his voice soothed their passions. They recognized him once more as their leader.

Luther comes back to Wit-tenberg,

The prophets came to visit him—and this is a proof of their sincerity—expecting him at once to admit their claims. Luther did not doubt that they were inspired.

but warned them lest their inspiration should and confronts the prophets.
come from Spirits of Evil. One of them,
with the voice and tones of an enthusiast, stamping
his feet, and striking his hands on the table, gave vent
to his horror at the suggestion ; and then, gathering
up his dignity, in a tone which almost shook the common sense of Luther, said solemnly, ' That thou mayst
know, O Luther, that I am inspired by the Spirit of God,
I will tell thee what is passing in thy mind.' And then as
Luther, really for the moment half carried away`by his
impressive manner, was beginning to waver, ' It is ' (he
added), ' That thou art ready to think that my doctrine
is true.' To which Luther, suddenly re- His common sense prevails.
covering himself replied, ' The Lord rebuke
thee, Satan! The God whom I worship will soon put a
stop to your spirits.' And with these parting words he
dismissed the prophets of Zwickau.

Order was restored at Wittenberg. The Scriptures
were again acknowledged as the rule of faith, and be-
fore the end of the year the New Testa- The prophets driven from Wittenberg.
ment was published in the German tongue.
The Lutheran Reformation was severed for
ever from the wilder reforms of Carlstadt and the
prophets of Zwickau; and the latter were soon driven
from Wittenberg, to spread their doctrines in other
places where there was no Luther to withstand them.

One of the disciples of Storch at Zwickau was *Münzer*,
but instead of going to Wittenberg, *he* went Münzer becomes the prophet of the peasantry.
first into Bohemia, and then all over that
part of Germany where Joss Fritz had been.
He became very soon the prophet of the
peasantry.

We must look even upon Münzer as honest and
sincere, though wild. He thought himself inspired, and

preached like a prophet. Along with many reforms
which Luther also urged, he claimed for the people the
right of having divine worship performed in their own
language instead of in the Latin of the priests. He
preached a crusade against all who opposed the gospel,
and urged a resort to the sword if preaching would not
do. Driven from city to city, he went more and more
among the peasants; and who shall blame him if he
took up their grievances? Was it not natural? His
own father, it is said, had fallen a victim to a quarrel
with his feudal lord. He began to think himself the
chosen messenger of heaven to avenge their wrongs;
and as he preached from place to place amongst the
peasantry, and others like him followed in his track, it
was not strange if it stirred up again in the minds of the
disciples of Joss Fritz recollections of the days of the
Bundschuh.

(*b*) *The end of Sickingen and Hutten,* (1523).

The council of regency appointed at the Diet of
Worms to represent the Empire during the Emperor's
absence in Spain (whither he had gone to quell a rebellion of his subjects) was made up of princes who had
more or less sympathy with Luther.

Frederic of Saxony was at the head of it. It was the
nearest approach to a central government which had
been formed. It was thoroughly German
and national in spirit, and aimed at thoroughly national objects. It aimed not at
carrying out the edict against Luther, but at
obtaining from future diets those reforms
which had been refused at Worms. It
aimed at putting down private wars and the establishment of public peace.

The Council of Regency under the Elector of Saxony strives to avert the storm,

But it had no power at its back to carry out its intentions. Its efforts to obtain something like union among the powers of Germany in the work of reform were fruitless; and so were its efforts to put down private wars.

Knights like Franz von Sickingen saw in it an attempt of the princes to put down the influence of their order. Its attempt to obtain the means to pay for national objects by a system of customs—duties on luxuries imported into Germany from abroad—was but meets taken by the merchants of the towns to be with opposition. an invasion of their rights. So it was unpopular and powerless, though its intentions were good.

Its powerlessness to preserve the public peace was soon shown in a great private war which was waged by Franz von Sickingen in 1522–3 against the Franz von Archbishop of Treves. The knight besieged takes to the Treves with his army of 5,000 foot-soldiers sword, and 1,500 knights, and declared that he came to bring the people freedom from the Pope and priests, and to punish the archbishop for his sins against God and the Emperor.

What could be a stronger example to the peasantry to take to the sword than such an act of the popular knight!

He counted upon the people of the town aiding him from within the walls, but was disappointed. The city held out till some neighbouring princes came to its rescue with an army of 30,000 men. On their approach, Franz retired to his castle of Landshut, there not being time to reach that of Ebernburg. There he was himself besieged. The cannon of the princes were powerful enough to batter down the solid walls, which before the use of

but is defeated
and killed.

artillery would have been impregnable. He
held out for months, till at last a solid tower
fell into a heap of ruins, and a breach was
made in the walls. Franz himself was wounded and
dying when his conquerors entered the castle. They
upbraided him for disturbing the peace of the Empire.
'I am going,' he said, as he lay upon the floor, dying,

Hutten's death.

'to render an account to a greater than the
Emperor;' and soon after he expired. His
friend Hutten died in the same year, while trying to urge
other knights to aid Sickingen, and this was the end of
the knights of Ebernburg Castle.

They had threatened to reform the Empire by the
sword. The peasantry had looked to them as their best
knightly friends. They had done much by their pens
and swords, their voice and example, to stir up warlike

The peasantry
got nothing
from the
knights.

feeling among the peasantry, but their end
came before the peasants had got any help
from them. In the meantime it was also
clear that the council of regency was unable
to preserve the public peace, as well as to bring about
the needed reform.

If help was to come neither from the Emperor and the
council of regency, nor from the knights, where were the
peasantry to turn next? Was not the time ripe for
rebellion?

(c) *The Peasants' War* (1525).

We must turn again to the map on which are marked
the districts where lay the smouldering embers of the
Bundschuh, waiting only for the match to light them up
again. On the opposite map are marked the districts in
which, one after another, the explosions came. The
connexion between the two maps will be seen at a

glance. Joss Fritz had kept the embers alive by his secret work in Swabia. The expulsion of Carlstadt from
Wittenberg had sent him into the towns on the Rhine
and in Franconia to stir up discontent and a spirit of rebellion, not only against Rome, the priests and monks,
but also against Luther, through whose in- Carlstadt and
fluence he had been expelled. Münzer had Münzer stir up
been driven from city to city, and thence rebellion.
into Southern Germany, to carry on the
work of stirring up rebellion.

The train was indeed laid, and in November, 1524,
the match was put to it in the very places where it
was laid the deepest. The match was a little thing.
The much-enduring peasantry of Swabia, and most of
all, those about the Boden See (Lake Constance) needed
but the last straw to break the back of their endurance.
It was a holiday, and the peasants on the estates of the
Count von Lüpfen were resting at home or taking the
day for work on their own land. Orders came from the
Count that they should turn out and gather Insurrection
snail-shells for the folk at the Castle. It was of the peasant-
the very littleness of the thing which made ry in Swabia.
it so unbearable. They rose up in arms, and so did
their neighbours in the valleys round. Soon all Swabia
was in insurrection.

The council of regency sent ambassadors to mediate
between the peasants and their lords of the Swabian
League. But it was of no use. They had not power to
keep the public peace. Neither party listened to them.
The peasants put forth twelve articles in which they
stated their demands. Here, in brief, is a list of
them. A mere glance will show that they were the old
demands of the days of the *Bundschuh*, with a few
additions.

1. The right to choose their own pastors.
2. They would pay tithe of corn, out of which the pastors should be paid, the rest going to the use of the parish.—But small tithes, *i. e.*, of the produce of animals, every tenth calf, or pig, or egg, and so on, they would not pay.

Their twelve articles.

3. They would be free, and no longer serfs and bondmen.
4. Wild game and fish to be free to all.
5. Woods and forests to belong to all for fuel.
6. No services of labour to be more than were required of their forefathers.
7. If more service required, wages must be paid for it.
8. Rent, when above the value of the land, to be properly valued and lowered.
9. Punishments for crimes to be fixed.
10. Common land to be again given up to common use.
11. Death gifts (*i. e.*, the right of the lord to take the best chattel of the deceased tenant) to be done away with.
12. Any of these articles proved to be contrary to the Scriptures or God's justice, to be null and void.

From this list of most substantial grievances we may well gather what the peasants were aiming at. We see how they aimed, like simple men, at the removal of the practical grievances and hardships of their life. But their demands were not at all likely to be granted. For instance, if they had the choice of pastors they would choose men like Münzer, and Carlstadt, and Storch, and perhaps even wilder spirits than these, so that neither the Pope nor Luther would be likely to concede that demand. Nor, of course, would the proud feudal lords like to lose their game and the forced labour of their serfs, and to meet their peasants on equal terms as free men, any more

Not likely to be granted by either Pope, nobles, or Luther.

than the slave-holders of America liked to have slavery abolished. We may guess, too, how the ecclesiastics would tremble to hear of their small tithes being taken away, and other pastors being chosen instead of themselves.

Had the feudal lords granted proper and fair reforms long ago, they would never have heard of these twelve articles. But they had refused reform, and they now had to meet revolution. And they knew of but one way of meeting it, namely, by the sword.

The lords of the Swabian League sent their army of foot and horsemen under their captain, George Truchsess. The poor peasants could not hold out against trained soldiers and cavalry. Two battles on the Danube, in which thousands of peasants were slain, or drowned in the river, and a third equally bloody one in Algau, near the Boden See, crushed this rebellion in Swabia, as former rebellions had so often been crushed before. This was early in April 1525. *[margin: Swabian peasants crushed in April 1525.]*

But in the meantime the revolution had spread further north. In the valley of the Neckar a body of 6,000 peasants had come together, enraged by the news of the slaughter of their fellow peasants in the south of Swabia. The young Count von Helfenstein, a friend of the Archduke Ferdinand, who had married a natural daughter of the late Emperor Maximilian, lived at the castle in the town of Weinsberg, in this district. He seems to have so far lost his head in these days of terror as to have cut the throats of some peasants who met him on the road. This enraged them the more. The town and castle were stormed and taken by the peasants, under their leaders, Florian Geyer, Wendel Hipler, and Little Jack Rohrbach. The *[margin: Insurrection on the Neckar, April 1525.]*

Count offered a large sum of money for a ransom, but the stern reply of the peasants was, 'he must die though he were made of gold.'

While the peasants were plundering the castle, the monastery, and the houses of the priests, the leaders held a council. Hipler advised moderation. He hoped that the smaller lords would, after all, side with the peasants. But Little Jack was a man of another kind. In the dead of night he held a council of his own, and doomed every knight and noble in Weinsberg to immediate death. As day was breaking the Count and other noble prisoners were led forth, surrounded by a circle of pikes with their steel points inward. The tears and pleadings of the Countess, with her babe in her arms, availed nothing. The peasants stood in two opposite ranks, with a passage between the points of their pikes. A piper of the Count mockingly led the way, inviting his late master to follow on a dance of death. The Count and nobles were compelled to follow. The ranks closed upon them, and they were soon pierced to death. A wild peasant woman stuck her knife into the Count's body, and smeared herself with blood. And so, un-

The peasants' revenge for Swabian slaughter.

known to the other leaders and to the masses of the peasantry, 'Little Jack,' on that terrible morning, had revenged the thousands of his comrades slain by the Swabian lords, blood for blood.

A yell of horror was raised through Germany at the news of the peasants' revenge. No yell had risen when the Count cut peasants' throats, or the Swabian lords slew thousands of peasant rebels. Europe had not yet learned to mete out the same measure of justice to noble and common blood. But the eye of history cannot so be blinded. It records that about a month after, Truch-

sess, the captain of the Swabian League, <small>The retaliation</small>
came northwards, and fell upon this band <small>of the nobles,</small>
of peasants with his more disciplined sol- <small>May 1525.</small>
diers and horsemen. One night, after a bloody battle,
in which several thousand peasants were slain, the piper
of Weinsberg was recognized amongst the prisoners—he
who had piped to the dance of death at the murder of the
Count von Helfenstein. Truchsess and the new Count
von Helfenstein, who was with him, had him fastened
with an iron chain about two feet long to an apple tree.
With their own hands they and other nobles helped to
build up a circular pile of wood round their victim, and
then they set fire to the pile. It was night; and amid
the groans of wounded and dying peasants on the battle-
field around them, and the drunken revelry of the camp,
was heard the laughter of these nobles as they watched
their victim springing shrieking from point to point of the
fiery circle within which he was slowly roasted to death.
Such was the revenge of nobles upon peasants.

But the revolution spread, and the reign of terror
spread with it. North and east of the valley of the
Neckar, among the little towns of Franconia, <small>Insurrection in</small>
and in the valleys of the Maine, other bands <small>Franconia.</small>
of peasants, mustering by thousands, de-
stroyed alike cloisters and castles. Two hundred of
these lighted the night with their flames during the few
weeks of their temporary triumph. And here another
feature of the revolution became prominent. The little
towns were already, under the preaching of Carlstadt
and such as he, passing through an internal <small>Revolution in</small>
revolution. The artisans were rising against <small>the towns of</small>
the wealthier burghers, overturning the town <small>Franconia.</small>
councils, and electing committees of artisans in their
place, making sudden changes in religion, putting down

the Mass, unfrocking priests and monks, and in fact, in the interests of what they thought to be the gospel, turning all things upside down.

A few extracts from the diary of a citizen of the free imperial fortified town of Rothenburg, on the Tauber, may serve to fix on the mind a clear impression of the Peasants' War, as it seemed to a citizen of a Franconian town during the course of the events which he noted in his log-book in this terrible year 1525.

Diary of a
citizen of
Rothenburg.

March 19.—The Carlstadt sect being favoured by the magistrates, Carlstadt himself came to Rothenburg, preached here, and wanted to become a citizen.

March 21.—Thirty or forty peasants bought a kettle-drum and went about proudly, insolently, and mischievously, up and down the city.

March 23.—About 400 peasants assembled.

March 24.—All citizens were called to the Rathhaus and enjoined to stand by the honourable council. Only twenty-six do so! The rest elect a committee of thirty-six. Messengers are sent to the peasants to inquire their plans. The peasants replied that they were not all collected yet. Letters come from Markgraf Casimir, and are read to the people, offering help, and to come in person to make peace. Some of the people treated the message with scorn and laughter.

This evening, between five and six, the head of the image of Christ on the Cross is struck off, the arms broken and the pieces knocked about the churchyard.

March 25.—The committee of thirty-six frighten the council into submission.

March 26, *Sunday.*—The priest driven from the altar and his mass book thrown down. The peasants deploy themselves before the Galgen-thor.

March 27.—The priest insulted, and his book thrown down whilst performing mass.

March 28.—700 peasants assembled, and force other peasants to join them.

March 31.—The peasants have increased to 2,000. Lorenz Knobloch having promised to be a captain, has gone out to them. Messengers from the Imperial Council came to make peace, but without result.

April 4.—The oil lamps thrown down during the sermon. The peasants go about plundering cupboards and cellars.

April 8, *Good Friday.*—The service done away. No one sang or read. But Dr. Drechsel preached against emperor, king, princes and lords, spiritual and temporal, for hindering the word of God.

April 10, *Easter Day.*—Hans Rothfuchs called the sacrament idolatry. No service.

April 11.—Dr Carlstadt preached against the sacrament. At night the Kupferzell (cloister) sacked by some millers, and tables and pictures thrown into the Tauber.

April 12.—Declarations made that priests may marry.

April 13.—Dr. Carlstadt preached again against the sacraments and ceremonies.

April 14.—Some women run up and down the streets with forks, pikes, and sticks, making a row and declaring that they will plunder all priests' houses.

April 15.—Priests are obliged to become citizens for safety. Every citizen to give a gulden towards the watch, also take his turn at working at the fortifications.

April 18.—The peasants demand 200 men and 100 long spears; a culverin, heavy field-pieces, and two tents. They are refused. The peasants reply that some citizens had promised help; therefore they now demand it.

April 23.—The peasants are told they shall have a reply in writing.

April 28.—Corn given out, but only some take it. Knobloch torn to pieces by the peasants, and they pelted one another with the pieces. The peasants have been heard to say that they would soon see what the Rothenburgers were going to do!

May 1.—In the night they burned the cloister of E., plundered another, and burned the castle of C.

May 8.—The people called together by the great bell in the parish church to hear a proposal of the Markgraf Casimir to come with his lady and jewels to Rothenburg; and on the other hand to consider whether to send to the peasantry or not.

May 10.—Three neighbouring cities have gone over to the peasants. They want Rothenburg to join them, too. At 6 o'clock people are called together again, and the majority decide to send artillery and spears to the peasants.

May 12.—More monasteries are sacked. Twelve kilderkins of wine plundered by the people and drunk.

May 15.—Florian Geyer (one of the peasants' leaders) in the parish church proposes articles of alliance with the peasants for 101 years. Demanded that the committee and people should by oath and vow league themselves with the peasants. Which was done, although against the grain to some. Thus to-day Rothenburg has gone over from the Empire to the peasants! A gallows was erected in the market-place in token of this brotherhood, and as a terror to evil-doers. About 5 o'clock tents, wagons, powder are got ready and taken to the camp of the peasants, with intent to storm the castle of Wurtzburg.

300 peasants who went up on May 9 to storm the castle of Wurtzburg were all killed, part by the stones, part shot, part slain —taken like birds! (So the castle still held out.)

Casimir of Brandenburg is marching with forces to chastise the peasants.

May 19.—He burns four towns. Four peasants at L. are beheaded and seven have their fingers cut off. At N. eighteen citizens beheaded.

May 27.—4,000 peasants are slain in the valley of the Tauber by the allied powers. (The combined forces of the nobles were now joined by Truchsess, who had been victorious over the Swabian peasants.)

May 29.—8,000 more peasants slain by the allies. Three messengers are sent from Rothenburg to Markgraf Casimir, carrying a red cross and fervently begging for mercy. No surrender would be accepted but on 'mercy or no mercy.' All citizens, clergy and laity, to pay seven florins for Blood and Fire Money, or to be banished thirty miles out of the city. The city to provide some tons of powder.

June 2.—Wurtzburg retaken by the Bund.

    •   •   •   •   •   •   •   •

June 24.—Mass said again, after thirteen weeks' interruption.

June 29.—Markgraf Casimir came to Rothenburg with 800 horse, 1,000 foot, 200 wagons well equipped with the best artillery, which are placed in the market-place.

June 30.—All citizens called by herald and ordered to assemble in the market-place, and form a circle under guard of soldiers with spears. It was announced that the Rothenburgers had revolted from the Empire and joined the peasants, and had forfeited life, honour, and goods. The Markgraf and many nobles were present. Twelve citizens were called out by name, and beheaded on the spot. Their bodies were left all day in the market-place. Several had fled who otherwise would have been beheaded.

July 1.—Eight more beheaded.

. . . .

It was during the Franconian rebellion that the peasants chose the robber knight Goetz von Berlichingen as their leader. It did them no good. More than a robber chief was needed to cope with soldiers used to war. The failure of the Franconian rebel peasants was inevitable, and the wild vigour with which they acted in the moments of their brief power did but add to the cruelty with which they were crushed and punished when the tide of victory turned against them.

While all this was going on in the valleys of the Maine, the revolution had crossed the Rhine into Elsass and Lothringen, and the Palatinate about Spires and Worms, and in the month of May had been crushed in blood, as in Swabia and Franconia. South and east, in Bavaria, in the Tyrol, and in Carinthia also, castles and monasteries went up in flames, and then, when the tide of victory turned, the burning houses and farms of the peasants lit up the night and their blood flowed freely.

Insurrection in Elsass and Lorraine put down, May, 1525,

and in Bavaria, the Tyrol, and Carinthia.

Meanwhile Münzer who had done so much to stir up

the peasantry in the south to rebel, had gone north into
Münzer heads   Thuringia, and headed a revolution in the
an insurrection town of Mülhausen, and became a sort of
in Thuringia.   Savonarola of a madder kind, believing
himself inspired, talking of his visions, uttering prophecies, denouncing vengeance on all who opposed what he
believed to be the gospel. He exercised over the citizens something of the influence that Savonarola had
done in Florence. His intense earnestness carried them
away. They could not help believing in him and regarding him with awe. For a while the rich fed the
poor, and under his eye there was almost a community
of goods. But Münzer, not content with visions and his
prophetic office, madly appealed to the sword. When
he heard of the revolution in Swabia, he seemed to
sniff the breeze like a war-horse. He issued a proclamation to the peasantry round about:

Arise! fight the battle of the Lord! On! on! on! Now is the
time; the wicked tremble when they hear of you. Be pitiless!
His mad   Heed not the groans of the impious! Rouse up the
proclama-   towns and villages; above all, rouse up the miners
tion.   of the mountains! On! on! on! while the fire is
burning; on while the hot sword is yet reeking with the slaughter!
Give the fire no time to go out, the sword no time to cool! Kill
all the proud ones: while one of them lives you will not be free from
the fear of man! While they reign over you it is no use to talk of
God! . . . Amen.
    Given at Mühlhausen, 1525. Thomas Münzer, servant of God
        against the wicked.

These were some of the words which were meant to
wake up echoes in the hearts of the neighbouring miners
of Mansfeld, among whom the kindred of Luther
dwelt!

. This was what had come of the prophets of Zwickau

giving up their common sense and following visions and inspirations!

But the end was coming. The princes, with their disciplined troops, came nearer and nearer. What could Münzer do with his 8,000 peasants? He pointed to a rainbow and expected a miracle, but no miracle came. The battle, of course, was lost. 5,000 peasants lay dead upon the field near the little town of Frankenhausen, where it was fought.

Münzer fled and concealed himself in a bed, but was found and taken before the princes, thrust Death of into a dungeon, and afterwards beheaded. Münzer.

So ended the wild career of this misguided, fanatical, self-deceived, but yet, as we must think, earnest and in many ways heroic spirit. We may well believe that he was maddened by the wrongs of the peasantry into what Luther called a 'spirit of confusion.'

The prince and nobles now everywhere prevailed over the insurgent peasants.

Luther, writing on June 21, 1525, says:—

' It is a certain fact, that in Franconia 11,000 peasants have been slain. Markgraf Casimir is cruelly severe upon his peasants, who have twice broken faith with him. In the Duchy of Wurtemberg, 6,000 have been killed; in different places in Swabia, 10,000. It is said that in Alsace the Duke of Lorraine has slain 20,000. Thus everywhere the wretched peasants are cut down.'

The struggle extended into Styria and Carinthia, where there had been risings before, and lingered on longest in the Tyrol. It was not till Truchsess was aided by the General George Frundsberg, the old general who had shaken hands with Luther in the Diet of Worms, that victory was secured to the higher powers.

Before the Peasants' War was ended at least 100,000

perished, or twenty times as many as were put to death in Paris during the Reign of Terror in 1793.

So ended the peasants' revolution. For two hundred and fifty years more the poor German peasantry must bear the yoke of feudal serfdom. They must wait till, in the beginning of the nineteenth century, German statesmen, awakened by the French Revolution, saw the necessity of preventing another Peasants' War by granting a timely reform.

Luther, throughout the Peasants' War, sided with the ruling powers. He was firm as a rock in opposing the use of the sword against the civil power. The reform he sought was by means of the civil power; and in order to clear himself and his cause from all participation in the wild doings of the peasantry, he publicly exhorted the princes to crush their rebellion. The peasants thought that in Luther (himself a peasant) they should have found a friend, but they were bitterly disappointed. He hounded on the princes in their work of blood.

The attitude of Luther during the Peasants' War.

That Luther should be bitter against Münzer and the wild prophets of revolution was but natural. He had seen the end from the beginning; he had left his retreat in the Wartburg four years before to quell the tumults at Wittenberg. Driven out of Wittenberg the prophets had become madder still. No doubt Europe owed much to the right-mindedness of Luther in setting his face against a resort to the sword in the cause of religious reform. Yet one cannot sympathize with Luther's harsh treatment of the peasantry and their misguided leaders. It cannot be denied that to some extent this revolution had grown up from the dragon's teeth that he himself had sown. There was a time when he himself had used wild language and done wild deeds. Erasmus had predicted that all Europe would be turned upside down in a universal revolution; and had it not come to pass? The monks blamed Erasmus and the new learning; Erasmus blamed the wildness of Luther; Luther blamed the wilder prophets. Who was to blame? History will not lay blame on Erasmus or Luther, or on the wilder prophets, or on the misguided peasantry, but on the higher powers whose place it was to have averted revolution by timely reforms. It was their refusal of reform which was the real cause of revolution. It was the conspiracy of the higher powers at the Diet of Worms to sacrifice the common weal to their own ambitious objects on which history will lay the blame of the Peasants' War.

Who was really to blame?

In the meantime let us not forget that there was one at least of the higher powers who had no share in the blame—one of them who had shown himself able to sacrifice his own ambition to the common weal, who had worked silently and hard for reform— the good Elector Frederic of Saxony. As the peasant rebellion under Münzer was going on in Thuringia, on the threshold of Saxony, he lay dying. He had no revengeful feelings. He did not urge on the slaughter of peasantry like Luther. He wrote to his brother, Duke John, who succeeded him as Elector, and who was gone with the army, to act prudently and leniently. If the peasants' turn had really come to rule, God's will be done! Only his servants were with him. 'Dear children,' he said to them, 'if I have offended any of you, forgive me, for the love of God; we princes do many things to the poor people that we ought not to do!'

Death of the Elector of Saxony, May 1525.

Soon after he received the sacrament, and died.

(*d*) *The Sack of Rome* (*1527*).

Now let us see what was the result to the higher
powers themselves of the secret treaty of
Worms, May 8, 1521, by which the Pope
and Emperor were to join their forces
against France, and to secure which the interests of the
German people were deliberately sacrificed.

Henry VIII. of England soon joined the alliance
against France. He had secret reasons to be mentioned
hereafter for keeping on good terms with
Charles V. and the Pope, and so had his
minister Cardinal Wolsey. Henry was tempted also
with the prospect of winning back the English provinces
in France, while Wolsey was flattered by the promises
of Charles V. to do all he could to get him elected Pope
on the next vacancy.

The first skirmishes took place between Charles V.
and Francis I. in the north, but with no decisive results.
Meanwhile the allied army in Italy was strengthened and
that of France weakened by the Swiss soldiers under the
pay of France being withdrawn, and Swiss recruits accepting imperial pay. The armies were soon in motion,
and on Nov. 25, 1521, Leo X. received tidings that the
allied army had triumphantly entered the
city of Milan, but while the rejoicings at
Rome in celebration of their triumph were still going on,
the Pope suddenly died, on December 1, not without
suspicion of poison.

To the surprise of everyone the Emperor's old tutor
was now elected Pope under the title of
Adrian VI. Charles V. had not used his
influence to promote the success of Wolsey. Adrian was
a Spaniard—a nominal governor in Spain while Ximenes
really governed—and was more likely to serve Spanish

interests than the wily English minister.   Adrian was a
sternly virtuous, well-meaning pope.   He would have
made peace if he could.   He would have reconciled the
German nation by reforms if he could, but with the wish
he had not the power.   Everything was against him ; he
was old ; his reign was short, and he died   Clement VII.
in 1523, to make way, not for Wolsey, for   Pope, 1523
again Charles V. played his own game, but for another
of the Medici, Clement VII.   He was not a Spaniard,
but the most powerful ally of Spain that Italy could produce among her cardinals.

In the meantime the Duke of Bourbon (one of the
Duchies which had become subject to the French crown)
rebelled from Francis I. and joined the im-   Duke de Bour-
perial league against France.   Henry VIII.   bon joins the
                                              league against
also was once more tempted by a vague   France.
prospect of again annexing French provinces to the
English crown, to help in the invasion of France.

The result of this invasion was to rouse the national
feeling, and therefore the power of France.   It was unsuccessful, and ended in Francis I. assum-   Francis I.
ing the offensive and crossing the Alps.   crosses the
                                           Alps.
Then came the battle of Pavia in 1524, in   Made prisoner
which the imperial armies under the Duke   at the battle of
of Bourbon and the old German general   Pavià.
Frundsberg gained the victory, and Francis I. was taken
prisoner.

Henry VIII. began now to dream not only of getting
back the lost English provinces, but even of being king
of France.   But Charles V. had little confidence in him
and Wolsey.   He was playing his own game, not that
of Henry VIII,

Pope Clement VII. meanwhile had expected Francis
I. to win at the battle of Pavia, and, to make himself

safe, had come to secret terms of alliance with him.
Before the battle of Pavia he had gone so far as almost

Rupture be-
tween Charles
V. and the
Pope.
to break with the Emperor. After the battle, all Italy began to be afraid that Spanish
influence would become omnipotent; so a
rupture between the Pope and Spain was
imminent. In the meantime the Emperor removed his
royal prisoner to Spain, so taking him out of the hands
of his allies. Then came the breach between Charles V.
and Henry VIII., the marriage of Charles—so long intended but kept secret—to the Infanta of Portugal, instead of to the English Princess Mary; the secret peace
of Henry with France. In 1526, followed the release of
Francis on his oath to observe conditions from which the
Pope at once formally absolved him. This produced a
final breach between the Emperor and the Pope, and an
alliance between the Pope and Francis against the Emperor.

It was at this moment that the Diet of Spires was
sitting. The Emperor had ordered that stringent mea-

Result at
the Diet of
Spires.
sures should be taken against the Lutheran
heresy, and that the Edict of Worms should
be carried out. This was impossible. The
new Elector of Saxony, and those who sided with him,
were too strongly backed for such a course to be taken.
Now the breach between the Pope and the Emperor came
to their aid. The Emperor no longer cared to back up
the interests of a Pope who had quarrelled with him, and
the result of the Diet was a decree signed by Ferdinand,
the brother of Charles V., in the Emperor's stead, containing the memorable clause, that 'Each state should,
as regards the Edict of Worms, so live, rule, and bear
itself as it thought it could answer it to God and the
Emperor.'

This left the Catholic princes to do as they liked on the one hand, and the princes who favoured Luther to do as they liked on the other. From this decree of the Diet of Spires came the division of Germany into Catholic and Protestant states.

This came out of the quarrel between the Pope and Emperor. The next thing was the gathering of a German army under George Frundsberg, an army composed almost entirely of Lutherans, under a Lutheran general, a host of discontented, wild, reckless men, who had survived the horrors of the Peasants' War, were inspired by hope of plunder, and inflamed by the zeal of Frundsberg, who declared, 'When I make my way to Rome, I will hang the Pope!'

March of a German army on Rome.

They crossed the Alps by a dangerous unguarded pass, descended into the plains of Lombardy, and then joined the Spanish army under the Duke of Bourbon. This was in January 1527. A few weeks more, and the combined army, 20,000 strong, was marching on Rome. Then came delays, rumours of a truce, and the mutiny of the Spanish soldiers for their long-withheld pay. Lastly, the German soldiers also mutinied, in vexation at which the old veteran general Frundsberg fell powerless under a shock of paralysis. The army advanced under Bourbon, and then followed the commencement of the siege of Rome; the death of Bourbon, shot as he was mounting a ladder; and—the rest shall be told in the graphic words, which the brother of the Emperor's secretary Valdez put into the mouth of an eye-witness in his 'Dialogue on the Sack of Rome.'

'The Emperor's army was so desirous to enter Rome, some to rob and spoil, others for the extreme hatred they bore to the Court of Rome, and some both for the one and the other cause, that the Span-

The sack of Rome.

iards and the Italians on the one side by scale, and the Germans on the other side by pickaxes breaking down the wall, entered by the Borgo, on which side stands the Church of St. Peter and the Holy Palace. Though those within had artillery and those without none, yet they entered without the slaughter of a hundred of themselves. Of those within were slain, some say 6,000, but in truth there died not upon the entry above 4,000, for they immediately retired into the city. The Pope in his own palace was so careless that it was a wonder he was not taken, but seeing how matters stood, he retired himself into the castle of St. Angelo, with thirteen cardinals and other bishops and principal persons who stayed with him. And presently the enemies entered, and spoiled and sacked all that was in the palace, and the like did they to the cardinals' houses and all other houses within the Borgo, not sparing any, no not the Church of the Prince of the Apostles ! This day they had enough to do without entering Rome, whither our people, hoisting up the drawbridge, had retired and fortified themselves. The poor Roman people, seeing their manifest destruction, would have sent ambassadors to the army of the Emperor to have agreed with him, and to have avoided the sack ; but the Pope would by no means consent to it.

'The captains of the Emperor presently determined to assault the city, and the very same night, fighting with their enemies, they entered, and the sack continued more than eight days, in which time they had no regard of nation, quality, or kind of men. The captains did what they could to stop it, but the soldiers, being so fleshed in their robberies as they were, you should behold troops of soldiers passing the streets with cries; one carried prisoners, another plate, another household stuff. The sighs, groans, and outcries of women and children in all places were so piteous that my bones yet shake to make report of them.. They carried no respect to bishops or cardinals, churches or monasteries; all was fish that came into their net; there was never seen more cruelty, less humanity, nor fear of God.

'They had no respect even to Spaniards and Germans, and other nations that were vassals and servants to the Emperor. They left neither house, nor church, nor man that was in Rome unsacked or ransomed, not even the secretary Perez himself, who was resident at Rome on behalf of the Emperor. Those cardinals who could not escape with the Pope into the castle of St. Angelo were taken and ransomed, and their persons full ill-favouredly handled, being drawn through the streets of Rome bare-legged. To make mocking of them, a German, clothing himself like a cardinal, went riding about Rome in his "pontificalibus," and a bottle of wine on the pommel of his saddle, and then a Spaniard in the same manner, with a courtezan behind him. The Germans led a bishop of their own nation (who stood upon election to have been a cardinal) to the market-place to be sold, with a bough in his forehead, as they do when they sell beasts.

'It is said that the sack of Rome amounted unto, by ransoms and compositions, above 15 millions of ducats. Churches were turned into stables. The Church of St. Peter, both on the one side and the other, was all full of horses! Soldiers carried along the streets nuns from monasteries and virgins from their fathers' houses, and from the time that the Emperor's army entered Rome till the time that I departed—the 12th June—there was not a mass said in Rome, nor all that time heard we a bell ring nor a clock. Not a priest or friar dared walk in the streets except in garments of a soldier, else the Germans would cry out, "A pope! a pope! kill! kill!'"

This was what had come to the Pope from the conspiracy of his predecessor with the Emperor at Worms,—
an imperial edict at the Diet of Spires, in 1526, leaving
the states of Germany virtually free to adhere to or sever
themselves from the ecclesiastical empire of Rome as
they severally pleased;—Rome sacked by a German
army in the Emperor's name, and more pitilessly pillaged
than it had been 1000 years before by the Vandals;—
the Pope a prisoner of the Emperor in the castle of St.
Angelo, and henceforth destined to act as the tool of his
imperial master, and to yield an enforced submission to
the supremacy of Spain!

Result of the   We may take this result as marking an
Papal policy.   epoch.   Rome had for ever ceased to be the
                capital of Christendom.   The old Roman
form of civilization radiating from Rome had finally given
place to a new form of civilization, which would go on its
way independently of Rome, and which Rome was no
longer able either to inspire or to control.

PART III.

RESULTS OF THE PROTESTANT REVOLUTION.

CHAPTER I.

REVOLTS FROM ROME.

IN SWITZERLAND AND GERMANY.

(*a*) *Meaning of Revolt from Rome.*

WE have now to trace how the Protestant Revolution resulted in several national revolts from the ecclesiastical
empire of Rome.

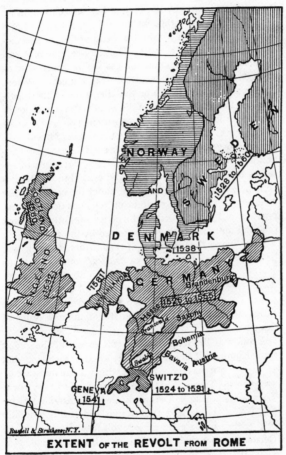

EXTENT OF THE REVOLT FROM ROME

M

But first, what did a national revolt from Rome mean?
It was the claiming by the civil power in each nation of
Meaning of re-
volt from
Rome. those rights which the Pope had hitherto
claimed within it as head of the great eccle-
siastical empire. The clergy and monks had
hitherto been regarded more or less as foreigners—*i. e.* as
subjects of the Pope's ecclesiastical empire. Where
there was revolt from Rome the allegiance of these persons to the Pope was annulled, and the civil power
claimed as full a sovereignty over them as it had over its
lay subjects. Matters relating to marriages and wills still
for the most part remained under ecclesiastical jurisdiction as before, but then, as the ecclesiastical courts themselves became national courts and ceased to be Roman
or Papal, all these matters came under the control of the
civil power. Even in matters of religious doctrine and
practice and public worship, the civil power often claimed
the final authority hitherto exercised by the Pope.

Such being the meaning of revolt from Rome, it will
be clear at once that it was a *political* quite as much as
A political
change. and sometimes more than a *religious* matter
—an assertion by the civil power in each
nation of that free independent national life
which we noticed as characteristic of the new order of
things.

A study of the map showing 'the extent of the revolt
from Rome' will illustrate this by another fact—viz. that
The Teutonic
nations revolt-
ed.
The Romanic
nations re-
mained
under Rome. it was those nations which in the main are of
Teutonic or German origin—Germany, Swit-
zerland, Denmark, Sweden, England, Scotland, and the Netherlands—which finally
made good their revolt from Rome. As the
Germans under their great leader 'Hermann' had, 1500
years before, been the first to make good their indepen-

dence from the old Roman Empire, so it was in the nations which were of Germanic speech and origin that revolt was made from papal Rome. On the other hand those nations—Spain, France, and Italy—which had long formed a part of the old Roman Empire, and were *Romanic* in their languages and instincts, remained in allegiance to the Pope.

There were no doubt many people in Spain, France, and Italy who sympathized with the doctrines of the Reformers, but there was no revolt, because these nations, or the civil powers representing them, chose to remain politically connected with Rome.

It is well to observe also how the turn the revolt took in the revolting nations was in a great degree the result of their political condition.

Thus in England, Denmark, Sweden, in which the central power was strong enough to act for the nation and to carry the nation with it, there was a decisive national revolt from Rome; while in Switzerland and Germany, where practically there was no central power capable of acting for the nation as a whole, there were divisions and civil wars within the nation, some of its petty states at length revolting from Rome, and others remaining under the ecclesiastical empire.

In some nations there was a national revolt. In some divided action and civil wars.

We will first take the case of these divided nations—Switzerland and Germany, and then pass on to the others.

(b) The Revolt in Switzerland.

No nation was so absolutely without a central authority as the Swiss. Each canton was as independent of the others for most purposes as the petty feudal states of Germany. When Machiavelli complained of the divisions of Italy

Switzerland divided into Cantons.

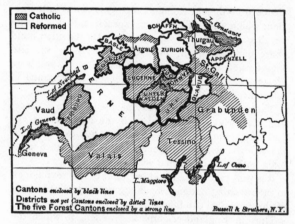

preventing its becoming a nation, he warned the Italians
of the danger of a country being 'cantonized' like Switzerland. But there was this difference between a Swiss
canton and a petty feudal state. In the Swiss canton
there was no feudal lord; the people governed themselves. It was not a feudal lordship, but a little republic
of communes or villages of the primitive Teutonic type,
in which the civil power was vested in the community.

Civil power vested in the people.

If therefore in a Swiss canton the civil power took to
itself the ecclesiastical power hitherto held
by the Pope, that power became vested in
the *people*, not, as in other countries, in the
prince or king.

Bearing this in mind, the history of the revolt from
Rome in Switzerland will be easily comprehended.

Ulrich Zwin-
gle, the Swiss
reformer.

The Swiss reformer, *Ulrich Zwingle*, was
born in 1484, and was the son of the chief
man of his village. Well educated at Basle

and Berne, and after having taken this degree at the
university at Vienna, he became a curate in Canton
Glarus. The new learning had spread into Switzerland,
and Zwingle was one of its disciples. He studied Plato
and the new Testament in Greek, like Colet and Erasmus. Being sent into Italy twice as army preacher, he
saw the Swiss troops conquered at Marignano, and re·
turned home full of patriotic hatred of the system of
hiring out troops to fight other nations' battles. Then he
settled in Zurich and became a reformer; Settles at Zu-
preaching against indulgences, celibacy in rich.
the clergy, and whatever else he thought could not be
justified by the New Testament.

His own canton, Zurich, under his influ- Zurich as-
ence, threw off the episcopal yoke of the ecclesiastical
Bishop of Constance and assumed the eccle- powers.
siastical authority to itself. The Zurich government au-
thorized the use of their mother tongue instead of Latin
in public worship, burned the relics from the shrines
and altered the mode of admistering the sa- Berne did the
craments. So Zurich revolted from Rome same soon
in 1524. Berne followed soon after; while after.
the *Forest Cantons*—Lucerne, Zug, Schwitz, Uri, and Un-
terwalden—followed by Fribourg and the Valais, which
was not yet a Swiss canton, held to the old order of
things.

Some cantons going one way and some another, the
result was division and civil war, the Catholic cantons
calling in the aid of their old feudal enemies, Civil war.
the House of Hapsburg. The civil war
lasted, off and on, for two or three years till, in 1531,
after Zwingle himself had fallen in battle, it was ended
by the peace of Cappel, at which it was Peace of
decided that each canton should do as it Cappel, 1531.

liked, while in the districts which were dependent on the
Swiss Confederation, and not to any particular canton,
the majority in each congregation should manage its
own ecclesiastical affairs.   The map will show which
cantons revolted from Rome, and how the districts were
divided in their action.

Zwingle was a true patriot.   He wished to see the
Swiss a united nation ; and with that object he proposed

Character of Zwingle.   political as well as religious reforms which
are now being carried out.   He was rather
a disciple of Erasmus than of Luther.   He did not adopt
the strong Augustinian views of Luther.   He also took
freer views respecting the sacraments.   Luther, a slave
in this respect to the mere letter of Scripture, held by the

*Luther quar-
rels with
Zwingle.*   words 'This is my body' so strongly as to
uphold the doctrine of 'the real presence'
almost as fully as the Catholic party.
Zwingle took wider views, treating the sacrament as a
symbol   The violent dogmatic intolerant spirit of
Luther was never more painfully shown than in the dispute with Zwingle on this subject.   The bitter hatred he
showed to Zwingle and Erasmus was all of a piece with
his violent feelings against the poor peasants of
Germany.   Whilst doing justice to the noble and heroic
character of the great German reformer, these things re-
mind us that there lingered in his mind much of the
dogmatism and intolerance of the scholastic theologian.

(c) *The Revolt in Germany* (1526–1555).

We have seen how the German people suffered at the
commencement of the era because they had not yet become a united nation ; and also how deep and widely
spread were their yearnings after national life and unity
—peasants crying out to the higher powers for protec-

tion from feudal oppression—Luther and Hutten appealing to them to free the German nation from the tyranny of the great ecclesiastical empire of Rome. Had Charles V. cared more for Germany than his own selfish ambitions, and put himself at the head of the strong national feeling, as Frederick of Saxony wanted him to do at Worms, there was at least a good chance of uniting Germany into a powerful and prosperous nation. But he threw away the chance. We have seen how the course taken by Charles V. and the higher powers in the Diet of Worms produced a revolution which cost a hundred thousand lives. We have now to see how it divided Germany into two hostile camps, hurried her into the horrors of the Thirty Years' War, postponed for eight or ten generations the freedom of her peasantry, and left to our own times the realization of the yearnings of the German people after national unity.

The freedom of the German peasantry postponed for ten generations.

The Diet of Spires, 1526, left each state to take its own course about Luther.

The decision of the Diet of Spires in 1526 had already settled that each state of the Empire should do as it thought best in the matter of the edict against Luther.

As might be expected, those princes who sided with Luther, and followed the lead of Saxony, at once took reform into their own hands. Monasteries were reformed or suppressed, and their revenues turned to good account, either for educational purposes, for supporting the preaching of the gospel, or for the poor. Monks and nuns were allowed to marry, Luther himself setting the example of marrying a nun. Divine service was in part carried on in German, though Latin was not entirely excluded. The

Hence arose Protestant states, with national churches free from Rome, while others remained Catholic.

youth were taught to read in common schools and in the language of the Fatherland. Luther's German Bible and German hymns came into popular use. In a word, in what were called the 'Evangelical States' a severance was made from the Church of Rome; and national churches sprang up, resting on the civil power of each state for their authority and adopting Lutheran doctrines. This was the result of the decree of the first Diet of Spires and the Emperor's quarrel with the Pope.

Meanwhile the Emperor, having settled his quarrel with the Pope, returned to his loyalty to Rome, and, taking advantage of this, the Catholic party succeeded, in the second Diet of Spires, in 1529, in passing a decree re-enacting the Edict of Worms, and forbidding all future reform till a regular council was summoned. The Lutheran princes protested against the decree, and so earned the name of 'Protestants.'

The second Diet of Spires, 1529, reversed the decision, notwithstanding the protest of the Protestant princes.

Civil war would very likely have at once resulted from this had not the Turks very opportunely made an attempt to extend their empire westward by besieging Vienna. The old dread which filled the minds of Christians at the beginning of the era came upon them again. Melanchthon, who, with all his wisdom, still believed in astrology, watched the movements of the stars, and augured disastrous results from the approach of a comet. Luther showed how thorough a German he was by counselling unity in the moment of common danger. For a time Germany was united again, but only till the Turks had retreated from Vienna.

Civil war averted by the Turks' attack on Vienna.

Charles V. had now reached the summit of his power. He had conquered France, he had conquered the Pope, he had been crowned king of Italy at Bo- The Turks driven back. Charles V. turns again upon German heretics. logna. He was now again reconciled with the Pope, and lastly, he had driven back the Turks. He had only to conquer the he- retics of Germany to complete the list of his triumphs. So he came in person to the Diet of Augsburg in 1530 to ensure by his presence the enforce- ment of the Edict of Worms. Every effort was made to induce the Protestant princes to submit; Diet of Augs- burg. The 'Augsburg Confession.' but, headed by John of Saxony and Philip of Hesse, they maintained their ground. Luther and Melanchthon were at Coburg, near at hand, and drew up a statement of Lutheran doc- trines which was known henceforth as the 'Augsburg Confession.'

The Emperor at length gave them a few months to consider whether they would submit; if not, the decree of the Diet was, that the Lutheran heresy Protestant princes form the league of Schmalkald for mutual defence. should be crushed by the imperial power. The Protestant princes at once formed the 'league of Schmalkalden' for mutual de- fence. And this, in spite of Luther's protest against opposition to the civil power, would have at once led to civil war, had not another Turkish invasion in 1532 again diverted the attention of Charles V. and of Germany from religious disputes.

During the life of Luther, the inevitable civil war was postponed. Melanchthon used the delay for an attempt, by argument and persuasion, to bring about a reconcili- ation between Catholic and Protestant theologians. At the council of Ratisbon, as we shall see Civil war postponed during Luther's life, by-and-by, a theological peace was almost concluded; but the schism was too wide and deep to be healed so easily. Meanwhile, state after state went over to the Protestant side, and civil war became more and more imminent. The death of Luther in 1546 was the signal for its commencement. The Emperor and Catholic princes, by means of Spanish soldiers,

but it begins now tried to reduce to obedience the princes
soon after of the Schmalkald league. They conquered
his death. the Elector John Frederic of Saxony and
Duke Philip of Hesse, the leaders of the Lutheran party, and proceeded to enforce by the sword a return to Catholic faith and practice all over Germany.

Charles V. now appeared in his true light as the Spanish conqueror of Germany. John Frederick of Saxony

Spanish con- and Philip of Hesse, the most beloved and
quest of Ger- truly German of German princes, were sen-
many. tenced to death, kept in prison, and brutally
treated. Germany, which Charles V. had sacrificed at the Diet of Worms to secure his Spanish policy, was now kept down by Spanish soldiers, and practically made into a Spanish province.

This was not the national unity which the German people yearned after; it was subjugation to a foreign yoke.

A few years of Spanish rule produced its natural effect—revolt of the German princes, alliance even with France! and then came, with strange suddenness, the defeat and flight of Charles V. He made an attempt to regain part of the ground which the French had taken, and then abdicated, leaving the empire to his brother Ferdinand, Spain and the Netherlands to his son Philip

Revolt of II. Then followed his cloister life, his
the Protes- strange remorse in consideration that he had
tant princes. not averted all these evils by the timely de-
Defeat of
Charles V.; struction of the heretic Luther at the Diet
his abdica- of Worms; and then at last the end of his
tion and
death. strange, brilliant, but misguided life in 1558.

The struggle of Charles V. with Germany ended in the *Peace of Augsburg* (1555), with its legal recognition of the Protestant states and its wretched rule of mock toleration—*cujus regio, ejus religio* —toleration to princes, with power to compel their subjects to be of the same religion as themselves! It was a peace so rotten in its

The Peace of Augsburg (1555), and its rule of mock toleration.

foundation that out of it came by inevitable necessity that most terrible chapter of German history, and perhaps of any history—*the Thirty Years' War*—which cost Germany, some say, half her population, robbed her citizens of the last vestige of their political freedom, confirmed the serfdom of her peasantry for two centuries more, and left upon some of her provinces scars which may be traced to-day.

Such terrible paths had the German people to tread towards national freedom and unity. Ten generations of Germans had to bear the curse brought upon them, not by the Reformation, but by those who opposed it—not by Luther, nor even by Münzer and his wild associates, but

Evils brought upon Germany by Charles V.

by the Emperor Charles V. and others of the higher powers who sided with him when he sold the interests of Germany and signed the treaty with the Pope on that fatal 8th of May, 1521, at the Diet of Worms.

CHAPTER II.

REVOLT OF ENGLAND FROM ROME.

(a) *Its Political Character.*

THERE were two points in which the revolt of England from Rome differed from the revolt in Switzerland and Germany.

(1) England was a compact nation with a strong central government; and so, instead of splitting into

In England the revolt from Rome was national,

parties and ending in civil war, revolted altogether, the king and parliament acting together, and transferring to the crown the ecclesiastical jurisdiction hitherto exercised by the Pope in England.

(2) In the Protestant states of Germany and cantons of Switzerland, a religious movement had preceded and

and came at first from political causes.

caused a political change; but in England the political change came first and the change in doctrine and mode of worship long

afterwards. The severance of England from Rome was not the result of a religious movement, but of political causes, which we must now trace.

(b) *Reasons for Henry VIII.'s Loyalty to Rome.*

Up to a certain point in his reign Henry VIII. held by

Henry VIII. defends the divine authority of the Pope, and writes a book against Luther in 1521.

the Pope and opposed Luther. At the time of the Diet of Worms he joined the league of the Pope and Emperor, not only against France, but also against Luther. Whilst the Diet of Worms was sitting, he wrote his celebrated book against Luther and in defence of the

divine authority of the Pope—for doing which the Pope rewarded him with the title of "Defender of the Faith."

His zeal in this matter was so eager as to surprise Sir Thomas More, who was now in Henry VIII.'s service. When the king showed him the book, and he saw the passages in defence of the divine authority of the Pope,

He tells Sir Thomas More of a secret reason for it.

More (who himself doubted it, and had hinted his doubts in his Utopia by making the Utopians talk of electing a Pope of their own) questioned with the king whether it was wise to write so strongly on that point. "Where-unto (More says) his Highness answered me that he would in no wise anything minish of that matter; of which thing his Highness showed me a secret cause whereof I never had anything heard before."

Thereupon More studied the matter afresh, altered his opinion, came to the conclusion that the Papacy was of divine authority, and held that view so strongly ever after, that at last he died rather than deny it. The reasons which made Henry VIII. uphold the divine authority of the Pope, are the clue to the history of the severance of England from Rome afterwards.

What were they?

We saw how the ruling idea of Henry VII. was to establish himself and his heirs firmly on the throne. Kings had hitherto had such precarious thrones that they lived in constant fear of rebellions and pretenders. We saw how Henry VII. relied greatly on his foreign policy and alliances to make his throne secure, and that the chief way of making these alliances firm, in an age of bad faith and Machiavellian policy, was by royal marriages. Henry VII. knew Ferdinand of Spain would tell lies or break his oath without remorse, but he also knew that if he could marry his son and probable successor to Ferdinand's daughter, Ferdinand would stick by him in close alliance in order to secure that his daughter might some day be queen of England. So Henry VII. had married his eldest son Arthur, Prince of Wales, to Cathe-rine of Arragon, and when Arthur died, had strained a point to get Catherine betrothed to his next son, Henry VIII.

Henry VIII.'s marriage with Catherine of Arragon.

Now there was a difficulty about this marriage. If the marriage with Arthur was merely a formal marriage, then

it was only an ecclesiastical matter, and the Pope's consent to Catherine's marriage with Henry might make all

Secret doubts
about its
validity. right.   But if it was a real marriage, then
the second marriage with Henry would be
clearly contrary to the divine law, as contained in the Book of Leviticus, where marriage with a
brother's wife was forbidden: and so, in that case, the
question would be whether the Pope could set aside the
divine law, and make lawful what it forbad.   To do this
must certainly be a great stretch of the papal power, and
it only could be justified on the very high ground of the
divine authority of the Pope.

The betrothal of Henry to Catherine was from the
beginning a miserable affair.   Its object was political.

Its unsatisfac-
tory beginning. It was his father Henry VII.'s doing while
he was a boy; and so doubtful, to say the
least, was its validity to those who knew all
about it, that to Henry VII.'s superstitious mind the death
of his queen seemed a divine judgment upon it.   He
even then, as we have seen, proposed to marry Catherine
himself, but Ferdinand of Spain would not hear of it.   A
bull was obtained from Pope Julius II., treating the question of the reality of the former marriage as *doubtful*, but,
notwithstanding the doubts, sanctioning Catherine's marriage with Henry.   The betrothal was completed, but
the wary monarch made his son sign a secret protest
against it as soon as he was of age, so that he might at
any time set it aside if the turn of political events made
it expedient to do so.   We must remember, however,
that some of these matters were court secrets, and would
never have been publicly known had not future events
brought them to light.

Upon the accession of Henry VIII. it was needful for
him to make up his mind about his marriage.   The

doubts and difficulties remained the same as ever to those who knew all about it, and it was not possible to dispel them. But the alliance with Spain was still considered important. And so the marriage with Catherine was concluded. The public were told that the former marriage had never been consummated, and that Henry VIII. was acting under the sanction of a Papal bull. This silenced talk out of doors, and the king smothered any secret doubts of his own, relying on the divine authority of the Pope. So the matter was concluded, and now for years had not been questioned again. When, therefore, Luther's attack upon the divine authority of the Pope was attracting attention every- where, we see that Henry VIII. had serious reasons of his own for defending it. He knew in fact that the validity of his marriage, and the legitimacy of his children's rights to succeed to the throne, depended upon it.

Its validity rested on the Divine authority of the Pope.

He had naturally been very anxious for an heir, so that his throne might be secure. Unless he had an heir, people must be thinking who will be king next, and plotting to succeed to the throne. Henry and Catherine had had several children, but all had died except one—the Princess Mary—who, at the time of the Diet of Worms, was a child of four years old. On her alone the succession depended, and Henry was anxious to secure it, as we have seen, by a close alliance with the Pope and Spain, cemented by the marriage of the Princess Mary to Charles V. Henry VIII. knew that the succession to the throne might at any time be made very precarious indeed if he should ever quarrel with the Papal and Spanish Courts.

Henry VIII.'s anxiety about it, and the succession.

And anxiety to keep on good terms with the Pope and Charles V.

An event which happened about this time showed how

keenly alive Henry VIII. was to these anxieties about
the successsion of the Princess Mary. He
startled the world all at once by the execution of the Duke of Buckingham for treason; for having his eye on the succession
to the throne. The Duke, it was said,
amongst other things, had been heard to
speak of the death of the royal children as judgments on
Henry and Catherine for their marriage. This was
enough to rouse Henry's suspicions, and so, after a
formal trial, he was found guilty of treason and beheaded as a warning to others.

Execution of the Duke of Buckingham for having his eye upon the succession to the throne.

(c) Sir Thomas More defends Henry VIII. against Luther.

Probably the secret which Henry VIII. confided to
Sir Thomas More had something to do with the doubts
about the validity of the marriage, and
opened his eyes to the fact how the succession to the throne and the safety of the
kingdom was involved in the divine authority of the Pope. It set him, as we have
said, studying the fathers until he came to
the conclusion that an authority which had long been
recognized, and on which so much depended, must have
divine sanction. Having come to this conclusion, he
was not likely to be made more favourable to Luther than
he otherwise would have been. We have seen that the
Oxford Reformers had from the first taken high ground
on the necessity of unity in the Christian Church. They
had also always been opposed to the Augustinian views
which Luther had adopted. They had agreed with
Luther in little but in the demand for a religious and
ecclesiastical reform.

Effect of knowledge of Henry VIII.'s se-cret on Sir Thomas More's mind.

Erasmus had refused to identify himself with Luther, and while defending him up to a certain point against the Papal party had urged upon him moderation.   This advice Luther had not followed, and now Erasmus held aloof from the Protestant struggle, urging moderation on both sides, preaching unity, and going on quietly with his own works, amongst which were fresh editions of his New Testament.

It is not surprising, then, that when Luther wrote his violent reply to Henry VIII.'s book, More should be ready to defend it.   He did so, and as time went on his zeal against Luther grew by degrees almost into hatred. As news of the wild doings of the prophets of Zwickau and the horrors of the Peasants' War were reported in England, More laid the blame on Luther.   He regarded him as a dangerous fanatic, scattering everywhere the seeds of rebellion against the powers that be, whether civil or religious.

He also urged, his friend Erasmus to write against Luther.   In 1524, on the eve of the Peasants' War, Erasmus did write a book against Luther's strong Augustinian views, in which he urged that they were sure to lead to all sorts of abuses in wilder hands.   In the year of the Peasants' War Sir Thomas More wrote an earnest letter to one of Luther's supporters in Wittenberg, charging the Lutheran movement with having lit the flame of sedition and set Germany on fire.

Reaction in the minds of Erasmus and More against Luther.

It is sad to see good and noble men like More hurried into reaction, and unable to see the good and noble points in a man like Luther, as well as his violence and errors.   But it was not unnatural.   He dreaded lest the heresies which had led in Germany to the Peasants' War, might spread into England, and lest heresy and

N

treason should again be joined as in the days of the
Lollards. His judgment was no doubt to some extent
carried away by his fears. But we must recognize the
sincerity and mental reactions such as these in the lives
of good men. Each class of Reformers we have seen
to be suspicious of those who went further and faster
than they did themselves. Honest men of the old school
blamed Erasmus for all that happened. Erasmus, they
said, had laid the egg, and Luther had hatched it. Erasmus, in his turn, blamed Luther's violent conduct and
language. Luther again denounced Münzer and the wild
prophets of revolution, as well as the poor deluded peasants. If this was natural, so was the reaction in the
mind of Sir Thomas More. We need not, however, re-
gret it any the less on that account.

(*d*) *Reasons for Henry VIII.'s change of Policy.*

Having thus seen that Henry VIII. from policy, and
More from conviction, were at this time strongly in favour of the Pope and his divine authority, the next thing
is to mark how long Henry VIII. continued of this
mind. The answer is, *just so long as his alliance with
Spain continued.*

During the wars of the Emperor, the Pope, and Henry
VIII. with France, Wolsey (now cardinal and legate,
and Archbishop of York, and soon after lord chancellor
Wolsey, the   also) was the war minister. It was he who
great war   knew all the mind of Henry VIII. and car-
minister of   ried on his secret negotiations with Charles
Henry VIII.
V. and the Pope. It was he who managed·
the treachery with Francis I., and made what prepara-
tion was needful for royal meetings, embassies, and
wars. It was Wolsey, too, who had to manage parliaments, and urge them to grant subsidies to pay for the

wars, and when he could get no more money from Parliament it was Wolsey who managed to get it by legal means, such as forced contributions from private persons called ' benevolences.'

More was a novice on the privy council, and holding Utopian views, often in a minority against Wolsey's measures. Once he was alone in disapproval of the great minister's plans. Wolsey hinted that he must be a fool. ' God be thanked,' replied More, ' that the king has but one fool in his council ! ' {.marginnote More opposed to the wars with France.}

It mattered little to the king or Wolsey what he thought, but More took care to let the king know that England's joining in the wars with France was against his judgment.

Wolsey's and Henry's confidence in Charles V. was shattered by degrees. First came the treachery of Charles V. in not helping to secure the election of Wolsey as Pope on the death of Leo X. and afterwards of Adrian VI. Then came the continuance of the war against France, under the Duke of Bourbon, who flattered Henry with hopes of regaining in case of victory the lost English provinces in France. Next came Pope Clement VII.'s fast and loose game with the allied sovereigns; and lastly, the battle of Pavia. Of these events we have spoken in a previous chapter. {.marginnote Charles V.'s treachery, And the Pope's.}

On hearing the news of the capture of Francis I. at the battle of Pavia, Henry VIII. proposed that he himself should be king of France and Charles V. marry the Princess Mary, so that in her right Charles V. might some day become lord of all Christendom. Up to this moment he had clearly not changed his mind. He still wished to continue the Spanish alliance, and was true to

Catherine and the Princess Mary. But just as his hopes were at their highest point they vanished for ever. Charles V. let Francis I. resume his throne on conditions which the Pope declared to be null and void. Charles V., instead of marrying the Princess Mary, married the

Henry VIII.'s foreign policy all at sea again. Infanta of Portugal, and Henry found himself betrayed. Charles V. and the Pope, on whose alliance so much depended, had now both escaped from his control. When, by the conquest of Rome, the Pope himself soon after became Charles V.'s prisoner and tool, Henry VIII.'s foreign politics were indeed all at sea.

(e) *The Crisis—Henry VIII. determines upon the Divorce from Catherine of Arragon.*

Now look at Henry VIII.'s position. Mary was still his only child. There had never yet been a queen on

Results of breach with Spain. the throne of England. He could no longer rely on Charles V. and the Pope. They at any time, and for political purposes, and in spite of Henry, could dispute the legitimacy of his only daughter. Once more the succession to the throne was uncertain, and in its nature the uncertainty could not be cured. What was he to do?

He resolved to take the bull by the horns, to divorce himself from Catherine of Arragon, to disinherit Mary, to

Political reasons for the divorce from Catherine. marry a young maid of honour, named Anne Boleyn, and to hope for other heirs to the crown. It was a bold policy, for marriage was a matter which belonged to the ecclesiastical empire, and so the divorce required the Pope's consent. Wolsey set his wits to work to secure the Pope's sanction to the divorce. He got his own ecclesiastical power as legate increased by the Pope, and Cardinal Campeg·

gio over from Rome to join him in deciding on the
validity of the marriage. He tried every means to secure the divorce required by Henry. He
had no notion of destroying in Henry's
mind the papal authority which as legate
he wielded in part, and as pope still hoped
some day to wield entirely. Had he succeeded in obtaining the papal sanction, there would have been no breach
with Rome. But he failed. The Pope, at the bidding
of his Spanish conqueror, made endless delays ; and Campeggio returned without having settled anything. At last, in spite of all
that Wolsey could do, Henry VIII. determined to marry Anne Boleyn, and took the matter into his own hands.

*Wolsey tries
to get the Pope
to grant a di-
vorce, but
fails.*

*Henry VIII.
takes the mat-
ter into his
own hands.*

This involved a deliberate breach with Rome and the
fall of Wolsey. Henry VIII. made up his mind to face both.

(*f*) *Fall of Wolsey* (*1529–1530*).

Cardinal Wolsey had been the very type of an over-
grown ecclesiastical potentate. Second to none but the
king, he had assumed to himself a viceregal
magnificence and state. And now that ecclesiastical grievances had come to the top, and, above
all, the king himself was quarelling with the Pope, Wolsey became a sort of scapegoat for both ecclesiastical
and papal sins. He was condemned formally for having
used his legatine and ecclesiastical authority contrary to
the royal prerogative. But the king had so far connived
at and sanctioned the very things for which he was now
condemned, and used them for his own purposes, that
he could hardly deal very harshly with his old minister.
He left him his archbishopric of York, to which he returned in 1530. There he resumed some of his old state,
but by his intrigues to obtain popularity amongst the

Fall of Wolsey.

Northern nobles again excited the fears of the court. Messengers were sent down to arrest him of high treason, and he was on his journey to London to answer the charge, when, seized by a fever, he died at Leicester Abbey, having given utterance to the famous words, 'Had I served my God as I have served my king, he would not have given me over in my gray hairs!' Henry VIII. was not conspicuous for gratitude to his ministers.

(g) *The Parliament of* 1529–1536. *Revolt of England from Rome.*

Wolsey was dismissed in 1529. Hitherto the chief ministers and lord chancellors of kings of England had

Sir Thomas More lord chancellor.

been ecclesiastics. This rule was now broken through. The Dukes of Norfolk and Suffolk were made chief ministers and Sir Thomas More lord chancellor. Lastly, a parliament was called.

A crisis had come in English history. The parliament of 1529 was to England what the Diet of Worms might

Parliament of 1529. A crisis in English history like the Diet of Worms in German history.

have been to Germany. The English Commons made use of this parliament, as the Germans did of the Diet of Worms, to make complaints against the clergy and the ecclesiastical courts. For a long time the people of England, like the Germans, had resisted the power of the ecclesiastical empire. The freedom of the clergy from the jurisdiction of the secular courts on

Complaints against the clergy and ecclesiastical abuses.

the one hand, the jurisdiction of the ecclesiastical courts on the other hand over laymen in such matters as marriages, probates of wills, and the distribution of property amongst the next of kin on the death of the owner, were real and long-standing grievances. The clergy, by their

ecclesiastical courts, harassed and taxed the people beyond endurance. The character of the clergy and monks
was also grievously complained of. Wolsey
had sought, as Cardinal Morton had done
before him, to reform these abuses. Himself a cardinal and legate, he had sought
powers from the Pope to repress the evils ;
to visit and even suppress some of the worst
of the monasteries and correct the clergy ;
and his scheme, partly carried out, was to
found colleges at the universities out of the proceeds.

Wolsey's
attempts at
ecclesiastical
reform under
papal autho-
rity.

The king
and parlia-
ment now
take up the
matter.

This was all very well as far as it went, but it never went
far enough to be of much use, and now the time of reformation under papal authority was passed. Both king
and parliament were in a mind to undertake themselves
the needed ecclesiastical reforms.

A petition, describing at length the ecclesiastical
grievances, was laid by the Commons before the king.
The king submitted it to the bishops, at the
same time requiring henceforth that no new
law should be passed by the clergy in convocation, any more than in parliament,
without his royal consent. The bishops tried

Petition of
the Com-
mons against
ecclesias-
tical griev-
ances.

to explain away the complaints, but before parliament
was prorogued acts were passed fixing at reasonable sums
the amounts to be demanded for probate of wills and
funeral fees, prohibiting the clergy from engaging in
secular business, or holding too many benefices, and
obliging them to reside in their parishes.

These were matters of practical reform, such as Colet
had urged in his sermon to convocation in 1511. He
had urged that the clergy in convocation
should take up these reforms, and reform
themselves. They had let eighteen years slip by without

Practical
reforms.

doing it, and now the bolder power of Parliament was over-ruling their feeble opposition.

Meanwhile the divorce question went into another phase. Cranmer now came on to the scene. He was

The divorce question laid before the Universities by Cranmer. soon to be the chief ecclesiastical adviser of Henry VIII. He consulted the chief universities of Europe on the power of Pope Julius to dispense with the divine law, and so upon the validity of the marriage with Catherine. The Universities gave their opinions very much according to the influence brought upon them. The English and French were most in favour of Henry VIII.'s views. The opinions were laid before parliament in 1531, but nothing further was done that year.

In its next two sessions this celebrated parliament

Further reforms. proceeded step by step with ecclesiastical reforms. The greatest of all legislative scandals, benefit of clergy, was curtailed. Payment of

The king declared supreme head of the Church of England instead of the Pope. annates to Rome was forbidden. Appeals to Rome were abolished. Heretics were still to be burned, but speaking against the Pope was declared no longer to be heresy. The king's assent was made necessary to ecclesiastical ordinances. The Pope's jurisdiction in England was abolished and transferred to the king. Lastly he assumed the title of supreme head of the Church of England, which was finally confirmed by Parliament in 1534.

The king marries Anne Boleyn. The revolt of England from Rome is now completed. The king meanwhile determined to deal with his own marriage. In defiance of the Pope, he married Anne Boleyn in January 1532-3. The marriage with Catherine was declared null and void by Cranmer, now Archbishop of Canterbury, and by act of parliament. Thus the breach with Rome was complete. England had, in fact, revolted from the ecclesiastical empire, by the joint action of king and parliament, and with the assent, however reluctant, even of the clergy.

(h) Heresy still punished in England.

Now it will be observed that all this came to pass without any change of religious creed, without England becoming Lutheran or Protestant. All the while heresy was a crime against which king and parliament and clergy were equally severe. The breach with Rome made no difference on this point, except that speaking against the Pope was no longer heresy. There was as stern a determination as ever to prevent the spread of heresy in England. Wolsey's dying advice to Henry VIII. in November 1530 was not to let the new pernicious sect of the Lutherans spread in England. Tindal, the noble single-minded Englishman to whom we owe the first translation of the New Testament into English, was all this while watched and tracked and persecuted from place to place as a dangerous foe. Fired with zeal by reading the New Testament of Erasmus, to give the English people access to its truths in the "vulgar tongue," he pursued his object with a heroism and patriotism which should make his name dear to Englishmen. Strange was it that one of his persecutors was Sir Thomas More, who, in his "Utopia," had expressed views in favour of religious toleration.

There had been no change of religious creed.

Heretics still persecuted, and among them Tindal, the translator of the New Testament.

It was just after the sack of Rome that More published his opinion that heresy, being dangerous to the state, ought to be punished in England, lest it should lead to similar results to those it had led to on the Continent. It was only a few

Sir Thomas More's zeal against heresy.

months after, that when, on the fall of Wolsey in 1529, he was made lord chancellor, he had to swear by his oath of office, amongst other things, to carry out the laws against heresy.   He became now, by virtue of his office, the public prosecutor of heretics.   The bishops were his most active police, and ever and anon poor men were handed over to him for examination and legal punishment.   The times were barbarous.   Torture was used in the examination of criminals and of heretics also, and, it can hardly be doubted, even in the presence of Sir Thomas More. Yet, in a certain way, More's gentleness showed itself even in persecution.   By the law of the land, heretics must abjure or be burned.   More tried hard to save both their bodies and souls.   He used every means in his power to induce them to abjure.   During the first two years of his chancellorship he staved off the evil day. Every single heretic abjured ; no single fire had yet been lit in Smithfield during his rule ; but, in the last six months of it, three abjured heretics relapsing into heresy were burned under his authority, the dying martyrs' prayers rising from the stake, "May the Lord forgive Sir Thomas More !"   "May the Lord open the eyes of Sir Thomas More !"

Strange was it that during these sad months, while More was persecuting others for conscience' sake, he himself had to choose between his own conscience and death.

(i) *Execution of Sir Thomas More* (1535).

We have seen that he had come to the conviction that the Pope was head of the Church by divine authority.

More himself has to suffer for conscience' sake. He had held his post of Lord Chancellor so long as the action of Parliament involved only the much needed reform of ecclesiastical abuses—till 1532.   But so soon as, in

1532, he saw the breach with Rome was inevitable, and that Henry VIII. would delay no longer, he resigned the seals and retired into the bosom of his home at Chelsea —that home which Erasmus had made known all over Europe as a pattern in respect of domestic virtue, culture, and happiness.

More had firmly told the king that he disapproved of the divorce, both before and after he was lord chancellor. He declined to be present at Anne Boleyn's coronation ; and when warned and threatened by order of the king, his brave reply was that threats were arguments for *children*, not for *him*. When the oath acknowledging Anne Boleyn as the lawful wife of Henry VIII. was administered to him, he refused to take it. Bishop Fisher alone among the whole bench of bishops did the same. More and Fisher were therefore sent to the Tower.' *More and Fisher sent to the Tower.*

Himself in prison for conscience' sake, More's thoughts turned to the heretics against whom he had been so zealous; and he left a paper for his friends warning them if ever, by reason of their office, they had to punish others, not to let their zeal outrun their charity. It was, perhaps, a confession that it had been so with him. He pondered also on the divisions in the Church, and expressed his hopes that after all there might be a reconciliation between Catholics and Protestants.

His wife visited him in prison, and reminded him of his home and his peril in not taking the oath. 'Good Mistress Alice,' he replied to her, 'tell me one thing: Is not this house as nigh heaven as mine own ?'

His beloved daughter Margaret Roper visited him often, and the story of his love for her and her daughterly affection for him, has become a favourite theme of historians, painters, and poets.

His trial, like that of the Duke of Buckingham, was a typical Tudor trial. It was not a question of guilt or innocence, but of state necessity. Anne Boleyn's star bein - in the ascendant, Sir Thomas More and Bishop Fisher must die.

This is Mr. Froude's account of More's death:

'The four days which remained to him he spent in 'prayer, and in severe bodily discipline. On the night 'of the 5th of July, although he did not 'know the time which had been fixed for 'his execution, yet, with an instinctive feel-'ing that it was near, he sent his daughter Margaret his 'hair-shirt and whip, as having no more need of them, 'with a parting blessing of affection.

'He then lay down and slept quietly. At daybreak 'he was awoke by the entrance of Sir Thomas Pope, who 'had come to confirm his anticipations, and to tell him 'that it was the king's pleasure that he should suffer at '9 o'clock that morning. He received the news with 'utter composure. "I am much bounden to the king," 'he said, "for the benefits and honours he has bestowed '"upon me; and, so help me God, most of all am I '"bounden to him that it pleaseth his Majesty to rid me '"shortly out of the miseries of this present world."

'Pope told him the king desired he would not use 'many words on the scaffold. "Mr. Pope," he answered, '"you do well to give me warning; for, otherwise, I had '"purposed somewhat to have spoken, but no matter '"therewith his grace should have cause to be offended. '"Howbeit, whatever I intended, I shall obey his High-'"ness' command."

'He afterwards discussed the arrangements for his 'funeral, at which he begged that his family might be 'present; and when all was settled, Pope rose to leave

Execution of Sir Thomas More.

'him. He was an old friend. He took More's hand
'and wrung it, and, quite overcome, burst into tears.

'"Quiet yourself, Mr. Pope," More said, "and be not
'"discomfited, for I trust we shall once see each other
'"full merrily, when we shall live and love together in
'"eternal bliss."

'So about 9 of the clock he was brought by the lieu-
tenant out of the Tower, his beard being long, which
'fashion he had never before used—his face pale and
'lean, carrying in his hands a red cross, casting his eyes
'often toward heaven. He had been unpopular as a
'judge, and one or two persons in the crowd were inso-
'lent to him; but the distance was short, and soon over,
'as all else was nearly over now.

'The scaffold had been awkwardly erected, and shook
'as he placed his foot upon the ladder. "See me safe
'"up," he said to Kingston; "for my coming down I
'"can shift for myself." He began to speak to the peo-
'ple, but the sheriff begged him not to proceed; and
'he contented himself with asking for their prayers, and
'desiring them to bear witness for him that he died in
'the faith of the holy Catholic Church, and a faithful
'servant of God and the king. He then repeated the
'Miserere Psalm on his knees; and when he had ended
'and had arisen, the executioner, with an emotion which
'promised ill for the manner in which his part would be
'accomplished, begged his forgiveness. More kissed
'him. "Thou art to do me the greatest benefit that I
'"can receive," he said; "pluck up thy spirit, man, and
'"be not afraid to do thine office. My neck is very
'"short; take heed, therefore, that thou strike not awry
'"for saving of thine honesty." The executioner offered
'to tie his eyes. "I will cover them myself," he said;
'and, binding them in a cloth which he had brought

' with him, he knelt and laid his head upon the block.
' The fatal stroke was about to fall, when he signed for a
' moment's delay, while he moved aside his beard.

' " Pity that should be cut," he murmured, " that has
' " not committed treason." With which strange words—
' the strangest, perhaps, ever uttered at such a time—the
' lips famous through Europe for eloquence and wisdom
' closed for ever.'

(*k*) *Death of Erasmus.* (1536).

The news of the Death of Sir Thomas More in 1535
reached Erasmus in old age and suffering from illness,

Erasmus
dies soon
after.

but labouring still with his pen to the last.
He was writing a book on the ' Purity of the
Church,' and in the preface he described
his friend as ' a soul purer than snow.' He lived only a
few months longer, died in 1536, and was buried in the
cathedral at Basle with every token of respect.

Not forty years had passed since Erasmus had first
met Colet at Oxford, and since the three Oxford students

The work of
the Oxford
Reformers
had pro-
duced great
results.

whom for the sake of distinction we have
called the Oxford Reformers, joined heart
and soul in that fellow-work which had
caught its inspiration from Florence. How
much had come out of their fellow-work !
Colet, the one who had brought the inspiration from Florence, had died in 1519, before the crisis came. But
even then the work of the Oxford Reformers was already
in one sense done. They had sown their seed. The
New Testament of Erasmus was already given to the
world, and nothing had so paved the way for the Protestant Reformation as that great work had done. Since
Colet's death, Erasmus and More had never met. Each
had taken his own line. More was driven far further

into reaction than Erasmus. After the Peasants' War and the sack of Rome, Erasmus still preached tolerance on the one hand, and satirized the monks and school-men on the other hand. And his satire was just as bitter in these later writings as it had been in the 'Praise of Folly.' But he too, like More, held on to their old hatred of schism, preached concord in the Church, and longed for a reconciliation between the contending parties.

(*l*) *Dissolution of the Monasteries, and Reform of the Universities* 1536.

The bitter satire of Erasmus upon the monks bore fruit sooner than he himself expected, and especially in England. The necessity of a thorough re-form in the monasteries was now every-where acknowledged, and there was no longer any reason to wait for bulls from Rome before beginning the work. The king was in a mood to humble the monks. The bishops and secular clergy had bowed their heads to the royal supremacy. The time now for the monks and abbots had come.

The work set a going by the Oxford Reformers goes on.

Within a few months of More's death, a commission was issued by *Thomas Cromwell* (the minis-ter who was now vicegerent of the new royal ecclesiastical authority), for a general visitation of the monasteries.

Cromwell, now ecclesi-astical minis-ter of Henry VIII., in-quires into the state of the monas-teries.

The popular complaints against them were not found to be baseless. Scandal had long been busy about the morals of the monks. The commissioners found them on inquiry worse even than scandal had whispered, and reported to Parliament that two-thirds of the monks were leading vicious lives under cover of their cowls and hoods.

Erasmus, in his 'Colloquies,' had spread all over Europe his suspicions that the relics by which the monks attracted so many pilgrims, and so much wealth in offerings to their shrines, were false and their miracles pretended. He had visited and described both the two great English shrines of 'St. Thomas à Becket' and 'Our Lady of Walsingham,' and had dared to hint that the congealed milk of the Virgin exhibited at the one was a mixture of chalk and white of egg, and that the immense wealth of the other would be of more use if given to the poor. The result of the royal inquiry convinced Henry VIII. that the 'milk of our Lady' was 'chalk or white lead,' and that Thomas à Becket was no saint at all, but a rebel against the royal prerogative of Henry II.

And into shrines and relics.

The result of the visitation was the dissolution at once of the smaller, and a few years afterwards of the larger monasteries, the monks being pensioned off, and the remainder of their vast estates being vested in the king.

Dissolution of the monasteries and destruction of shrines.

The universities as well as the monasteries were visited by the Commissioners, and that reform was carried out at the universities which Colet, forty years before, had begun at Oxford; a reform which converted them from schools of the *old* into schools of the *new* learning. 'The learning of the wholesome doctrines of Almighty God and the three tongues, Latin, Greek, and Hebrew, which be requisite for the understanding of Scripture,' were specially enjoined, while the old scholastic text-books became waste paper and were treated as such.

Reform of the Universities.

These were the final labors of the memorable Parliament which begun in 1529, accomplished the revolt from Rome, and was now dissolved in 1536.

Parliament of 1529–36 dissolved.

One step further the Reformation went under Cranmer and Cromwell. In 1536 the Scriptures themselves, in the English translation of Tindal, revised and completed by Coverdale, were ordered to be placed in every church, and the clergy were instructed to exhort all men to read them. Thus England owes the basis of her noble translation of the Bible to William Tindal. He lived to see it thus published by royal authority, but soon after fell a victim to persecution in Flanders, and ended his heroic life in a martyr's death.

Tindal's translation of the Bible sanctioned.

Martyrdom of Tindal.

(m) *Later Years of Henry VIII.* (1536–1547).

In 1536 Queen Catherine died, and in the same year the still more miserable Anne Boleyn was divorced, and, with the partners of her alleged guilt, beheaded.

Execution of Anne Boleyn.

The sole offspring of this ill-fated marriage was the Princess *Elizabeth*, and she now, like the Princess Mary, was declared illegitimate, and thus the succession was again uncertain.

To meet this difficulty the king married his third queen, *Jane Seymour*, and parliament settled the succession upon her offspring, and in default of a direct heir, upon such person as Henry VIII. should name in his will.

Henry VIII. marries Jane Seymour.

Meanwhile, this time of renewed unsettlement was chosen by the papal party for a general rebellion, known as '*The Pilgrimage of Grace.*' Reforms had gone too fast for many. It was not to be expected that so great a change should meet with no opposition. It would have been strange if Sir Thomas More and Bishop Fisher had

A Catholic rebellion breaks out in the North,

o

been the only martyrs on the papal side. The rebellion
was chiefly in Lincolnshire and Yorkshire. It was headed
by some of the old aristocracy, and nó doubt was fo-
fomented by mented by the issue just before of a papal
the Pope and bull of excommunication against Henry
Reginald Pole. VIII., and by expectations of foreign aid.
Reginald Pole, a relation of the king's, and afterwards
legate and Cardinal Archbishop óf Canterbury under
Queen Mary, did his best, under papal encouragement,
to bring about a holy war against England, and thereby
It is quelled. enforce obedience to the papal power. But
these schemes of war from without came to
nought, and the insurrection within was promptly met
and quelled. The royal supremacy was vindicated by
the execution of the chief rebels, and the Catholic reaction thus postponed till the days of Queen Mary.

Probably the birth at this moment of a long-desired
prince (afterwards *Edward VI.*), did as much as the
Birth of execution of the rebels to assure the stability
Edward VI., of Henry's throne. But it cost the life of the
and death of
the Queen. queen-mother, and made another marriage
a state necessity. While Cromwell was pursuing his
Henry VIII. policy, dissolving the remaining monasteries,
marries demolishing the shrines of Walsingham and
Anne of
Cleves, Canterbury, and transferring their wealth to
the royal exchequer, he had once more to arrange a
match for Henry. His choice fell upon *Anne of Cleves,* a
connexion of the Elector of Saxony. It fell in with Cromwell's policy to use the opportunity to bring about a Protestant alliance, and Henry married in 1539 Anne of Cleves.

But how was it likely that he should fall in love with
a fourth wife who was plain-looking and spoke not a word
but does not of English? He soon was weary of his new
like her. match, and as Wolsey was sacrificed to se-

cure the divorce of Catherine, so Cromwell was now sacrificed to secure a divorce from Anne of Cleves. Another Tudor trial, with less show of justice even than those of the Duke of Buckingham and Sir Thomas More, paved the way for the state necessity. Cromwell, like Cranmer, had been all along half a Protestant at heart. Unless he had been, he could hardly have carried through as he did for the king, the successful revolt of England from the ecclesiastical empire of Rome. The king had profited by that, but he now meant to profit by Cromwell's fall. So Cromwell died upon the scaffold as a traitor.

Cromwell sacrificed to get rid of her.

Henry was soon rid of Anne of Cleves. The Protestant alliance fell through. A sort of reconciliation was made with Charles V., who naturally hated Cromwell more even than he had distrusted Wolsey. And a sort of colour of religion was given to the whole proceeding by the more stringent repression of those heresies towards which the fallen minister was said to have been unduly lenient. This was in 1540.

Reconciliation with Charles V.

The king now married the guilty, and unfortunate Catherine Howard, whose turn to die on the scaffold came (so soon!) in 1542; and then at last came the final marriage with Catherine Parr, a virtuous widow, who proved an honourable and efficient royal nurse during the king's few remaining years.

Henry VIII.'s last two marriages.

These years of his decaying health were marked by the renewal of the alliance with Charles V. and breaches of peace with Francis I. Henry's foreign policy ended as it had begun under the shadow of Spanish ascendancy, threatened English invasion of France, French retaliative invasion

Alliance with Spain, and wars with France.

of England, and financial difficulties which always followed in the wake of war. The treasures of Henry VII.
sufficed not to supply the means for Henry VIII.'s

Want of
money.

early wars with France. So again, in spite
of the wealth which came to the Crown from
the dissolution of monasteries and the destruction of the
shrines, the king in his last years found himself with an
empty exchequer, and obliged to debase the coinage to

Death of
Henry VIII.
in 1547.

obtain the supplies he wanted. He died in
Jan. 1547—the year after the death of Luther,
just as civil war broke out in Germany, and
Charles V. set about conquering Germany with his
Spanish soldiers.

While Germany was passing through this struggle,
England was becoming more and more Protestant, under

Reform goes
on during
the reign of
Edward VI.

the guidance of Cranmer, who managed the
ecclesiastical affairs of England in the short
reign of Edward VI.

But a reaction was to follow. On Edward VI.'s death

Catholic
reaction under
Queen Mary.

in 1553 the Princess Mary became queen.
A Catholic herself, and the wife of Philip II.
of Spain, she restored the Catholic faith in
England, and tried to quench the English Protestant
spirit in blood. But she died in 1558—the same year as

England be-
comes finally
Protestant
under Queen
Elizabeth.

Charles V.—and under her successor, the
Protestant Queen Elizabeth, the revolt of
England from Rome became once for all an
established fact. Thenceforth, both in politics and in doctrine, England was a Protestant state.

(*n*) *Influence of Henry VIII.'s reign on the English Constitution.*

It has been sometimes said that Henry VIII.'s reign
was the reign of a tyrant, and that during his reign the

English parliament was subservient and cringing to the monarch.

How far the constitution was maintained.

To judge of this matter rightly we must remember that England was passing through a great crisis in her history which we have likened to that which was marked by the Diet of Worms in German history. How different the English from the German result! At the Diet of Worms the Emperor and princes acted in opposition to the German people; the necessary reforms were not made, and so there came revolution. In

The revolt from Rome accomplished by constitutional means.

the parliament of 1529–36 the king and House of Commons acted together, and made the necessary reforms; the clergy submitted to them when they saw they must, the dissolution of the monasteries removed the abbots from the House of Lords and placed the lay lords in a majority, and so in the end England was forced from the yoke of the ecclesiastical empire of Rome by constitutional means, without the revolutions and civil wars which followed in Germany.

That such a revolution was peaceably wrought by parliament under the guidance of the king's ministers, Cromwell and Cranmer, sustained by most important precedents the power of parliament in the constitution.

The power of parliament maintained.

During his wars, Henry VIII.'s ministers, especially Wolsey, resorted to benevolences and forced loans to obtain supplies. But the fall of Wolsey, and on later occasions the sanction of parliament, obtained afterwards by way of in-

It preserved its control over taxation.

demnity for acts admitted to be illegal, kept up the constitutional principle that the king could levy no taxes without the consent of parliament. The real struggle on this matter came in the days of the Stuarts.

The new ecclesiastical powers of the king as supreme head of the Church gave rise to new branches of juris-

And over the making of new laws.

diction, some of which were of a dangerous kind. Parliament also, by statute, gave to the king's proclamation, within a very re- stricted range, the force of statutes, but this was repealed in the next reign. And on the whole, the second great constitutional principle on which English freedom is based was well maintained; viz., that the king could make no new laws without consent of parliament,

Bearing these things in mind it would be hard to deny that the parliaments of Henry VIII. deserve

On the whole the parliaments of Henry VIII. deserve well of Englishmen.

tolerably well of Englishmen, considering the greatness of the crisis through which the bark of the state had to be steered in their time.

The greatest blots upon the reign of Henry VIII. were the unjust trials for treason by which the most faithful

Unjust State trials the chief blot on the reign of Henry VIII.

of ministers were sacrificed to clear away obstacles to royal policy, and the way that sometimes justice was sacrificed to the per- sonal wishes or even passions of the king in connexion with his unhappy matrimonial caprices.

These things will always stain the memory of Henry VIII., but regarding his reign as a whole it would be

England fared much better than France and Spain.

unfair to forget that in it a great crisis was passed through without civil war, which left England freed from the ecclesiastical em- pire of Rome, and under a constitutional monarchy, while France and Spain were left to struggle for cen- turies more under the double tyranny of the ecclesiasti- cal empire and their own absolute kings.

CHAPTER III.

REVOLT OF DENMARK AND SWEDEN AND (LATER) OF THE NETHERLANDS.

(a) *Denmark and Sweden (1525–1560).*

DENMARK and Sweden both revolted from Rome, but under peculiar circumstances. From 1520 to 1525 they had both been governed by one king—a wretched tyrant—Christian II., who legally had little power, but following the royal fashion of the day, tried to make himself an absolute monarch. Denmark and Sweden both rebelled, dethroned Christian II., and then went their several ways. Both Denmark and Sweden throw off the yoke of Christian II. and then separate.

In Sweden the people, *i. e.* the citizens and then the peasantry, were sick of the tyranny of their nobles and clergy, as well as their king, and sighed for a good king strong enough to curb them. It was the old story, what the citizens and peasantry of Germany had long sighed for in vain. But in Sweden they got what they wanted. They elected as king *Gustavus Vasa*, a noble who had taken the popular side against their former tyrant ; and having elected him, they backed him in carrying out in Sweden very much the same sort of reforms as Henry VIII. had carried out in England. The clergy were humbled, their property seized by the crown, The Swedes elect Gustavus Vasa their king. Sweden, under him, becomes a Protestant nation. and Sweden, roused to a sense of national life under Gustavus Vasa, took its place among modern nations. It was soon to play a prominent part in the great struggle between Catholic and Protestant powers. The Swedish king, *Gustavus Adolphus*, was the greatest of the Protestant leaders in the Thirty Years' War.

In Denmark also (and Norway was under the same crown) a new monarchy succeeded to that of the ex-
pelled tyrant. The nobles joined the crown in crushing the power of the clergy. The Danish monarchy became established on the ruins of the Church. Lutheranism was encouraged. Denmark became a Protestant state, and took part, like Sweden, on the Protestant side in the Thirty Years' War.

Denmark also, under her new king, becomes Protestant.

(b) The Revolt of the Netherlands (1581).

The last of the revolts from Rome was that of the Netherlands. It was a revolt not only from Rome but also from Spain. It does not fall altogether within the limits of the era, and so requires only brief notice here.

Philip II., king of Spain and husband of the English queen Mary, tried to enforce the double yoke of Spain and Rome upon the Netherlanders. The Netherlands, it will be remembered, belonged to the Burgundian pro-
vinces which came to the Spanish crown by the marriage alliance of the mother of Charles V. He was a Netherlander, and as such popular; but his son, Philip II., was a Spaniard, and felt to be a foreign tyrant. He had entered into close alliance with Rome. If he could, he would have conquered all countries which had revolted from Rome; and in restoring them to Rome, he would have liked to have made them into Spanish provinces. It was in pursuance of these ideas that he encouraged Queen Mary's restoration of the Catholic faith in England, and sent his 'Spanish Armada' to conquer the Protestant Queen Elizabeth. In the same spirit he sent his cruel minister, the Duke of Alva, to force into submission his rebellious subjects in the Netherlands, and to fasten on their necks the double

Policy of Philip II to subject the Nether-landers to Spain and to Rome.

yoke of Spain and Rome. The result was
the revolt of the Netherlands under the
Prince of Orange. After a terrible struggle, it was at last successful, and ended in
the complete escape of the northern provinces from both the Spanish and Papal yoke. This
was in 1581. From that date the 'United Provinces'
took their place, like Sweden and Denmark, among the
Protestant nations of Europe.

They revolt, and the 'United Provinces become a Protestant nation.

CHAPTER IV.

THE GENEVAN REFORMERS.

(*a*) *Rise of a new School of Reform.*

THE force of the Protestant Revolution was not wholly
spent in these national revolts from Rome.

Although apart from them there was a Protestant
movement going on in the minds of the people, both in those nations which revolted
from Rome and in those which did not.

A Protestant movement which was not national,

We must now turn our attention to the rise of a new
school of reform, which led to remarkable results.
Luther was too national—too German—a reformer, to
admit of his becoming the universal prophet
of Protestantism all over the world. Denmark, Sweden, and Norway, coming under
German influence, did indeed become
Lutheran; but the Protestants of France,
England, Scotland, and America are not
and never have been Lutherans. They
came more under the influence of the Genevan reformers, of whom we must now speak.

but which influenced the Protestants of France, England, Scotland, and America more than Luther did.

(*b*) *John Calvin.*

The chief of these was *John Calvin.* He was a Frenchman, born in 1509, and so was twenty-five years younger than Luther. He was educated at the universities of Paris and Orleans, adopted the Augustinian theology, as Wiclif, Huss, and Luther had done before him, and became a Protestant. In France heretics were burned, so he left his home to travel in Italy and Germany. In 1536, just as Erasmus was passing to his rest, he came to Basle, and began his public work as a Protestant reformer by publishing his 'Institutes of the Christian Religion.' It was these 'Institutes' of Calvin which gave rigid logical scholastic form to those Augustinian doctrines which, as we have said, were held in common by most Protestant reformers from Wiclif to Luther, but which have been since called 'Calvinistic.' He differed from Luther both in theory and practice, on those points about which Zwingle and Luther had quarrelled. He rejected transubstantiation, which Luther did not altogether; and he founded his Church, like Zwingle, on the republican basis of the congregation rather than, as Luther did, on the civil power of the prince. He thus was in a sense more Protestant than Luther, though at that time only the Lutherans were called Protestants.

Geneva soon became the sphere of his actions. It was in a state of anarchy, having rebelled from its bishop, who had been practically both ecclesiastical and civil ruler in one. Other French reformers had settled at Geneva before Calvin, and these shared his stern Protestant doctrines. But Calvin soon proved the most powerful preacher. Like

[Marginal notes:]

John Calvin, born 1509.

His 'Institutes,' which gave logical form to the 'Calvinistic' doctrines.

Calvin settles at Geneva.

Savonarola, he rebuked the vices of the people from the pulpit. At first this made him unpopular, and he was driven away; but in 1541 he was recalled by the people, and made practically both civil and religious dictator of the little state.

Becomes a kind of dictator of the Genevan state.

He was in a sense Protestant Pope of Geneva, but deriving his power from the congregation. He and his consistory held it their duty to force men to lead moral lives, go to church, give up dice, dancing, swearing, and so forth; and the council of the city supported this severe exercise of ecclesiastical power by their civil authority. Thus for twenty years Geneva was under the rule of Calvin and his fellow 'saints;' and an intolerant despotic rule it was. Men were excommunicated for insulting Calvin, and sent to prison for mocking at his sermons. To impugn his doctrine was death or banishment. Hired spies watched people's conduct, and every unseemly word dropped in the street came to the ear of the elders. Children were liable to public punishment for insulting their parents, and men and women were drowned in the Rhone for sensual sins. Witchcraft and heresy were capital crimes; and one heretic, Servetus, was burned, with his books hung to his girdle, for honest difference of opinion from Calvin on an abstruse point of divinity.

His severe discipline and intolerance.

The same view of the functions of the Church which led him to exercise this severe discipline, led him also to control education. He founded academies and schools; and when his system was applied to Scotland, as it afterwards was under John Knox, a school as well as a church was planted in every parish.

He founds schools.

(c) Influence of the Genevan School on Western Protestantism.

Whatever Calvin did at Geneva would have mattered little to the world if it had stopped there; but it did not. The historical importance of Calvin lies in the fact that he impressed upon Western Protestantism his rigid scholastic creed and his views of ecclesiastical discipline.

His influence on Western Protestantism.

The Protestants of France, called Huguenots, were and are mainly the offspring of Calvinism. John Knox, the reformer of Scotland, and the Scotch Covenanters, were also disciples of Calvin; and so Scotch Protestantism received its impress from Geneva. The Puritans of England were also Calvinists. Cromwell was a Calvinist, and the rule of his 'saints' was on the Genevan model. The Pilgrim Fathers took with them from England to the New England across the Atlantic the Calvinistic creed, and, alas! its intolerance too. So engrained was it in their theological mind that, even though themselves fleeing from persecution, they themselves persecuted in the land of their refuge. Under the rule of the Boston saints there was as little religious liberty as under the rule of Calvin at Geneva.

The French Huguenots, the Scotch Covenanters, the English Puritans, the 'Pilgrim Fathers' of New England, all of the Genevan school.

Nevertheless, the offspring of the Genevan school of reform deserve well of history. However narrow and hard in their creed and Puritanic in their manners, they were men of a sturdy Spartan type, ready to bear any amount of persecution and to push through any difficulties, democratic in their spirit and aggressive in their zeal. The banishment of the Huguenots from

Their historical importance, and influence on national character.

France took away the backbone of her religious life.
Scotland would not be what she is but for Knox and his
parish schools.   England could not afford to lose the
Puritan blood which mixes in her veins.   New England
owes a rich inheritance of stern virtues to her 'Pilgrim
Fathers.'

CHAPTER V.

REFORM WITHIN THE CATHOLIC CHURCH.

(*a*) *The Italian Reformers* (*to* 1541).

ONE of the results of the Protestant revolution was the
reform of the Catholic Church itself.

We ought never to forget that the Roman Catholic
Church of our own times is, in fact, a reformed Church
as well as the Protestant Churches.   And we must now
have patience enough to trace how and by whom its reform was effected.

Good men of all parties had for long seen the necessity of a practical reform in the morals of the pope, clergy,
and monks.   And we have seen that the necessity was
recognized in high quarters.   Ferdinand and Isabella's
great minister, Cardinal Ximenes, and the English ministers, Cardinal Morton and Cardinal Wol- Efforts at
sey—three cardinals all of great power and reform with-
undoubted loyalty to Rome—even went so Church.
far as to get bulls from the Pope, authorizing them to visit
and reform the monasteries.   All good men cried out
against the crimes of such a pope as Alexander VI.   And
it is not right to charge the Catholic Church wholesale
with these crimes any more than it would be to charge the
English nation with the matrimonial sins of Henry VIII.

There was so strong a feeling all through the Church

against these scandals that, after what had happened,

Improvement in the character of popes. they were not likely to occur again. The popes who came after Alexander VI. were not angels, but they were outwardly more decent than he, at all events. Julius II., as we have seen, was the fighting pope. The scandal in his case was his lust of war and the extension of the Papal territory. Leo X. cared more for art and literature than for war, but he, too, had his faults, and the scandal in his case was a doubt whether, after all, he really believed in Christianity. Adrian VI. was an earnest and stern moral reformer—too stern for the times—and his reign was too short to produce much result. Clement VII. was a better man than many, though of blundering politics, letting down the Papal power, and becoming at last the prisoner and the tool of his Spanish conqueror Charles V.

All this while there were men in Italy of earnest Christian feeling who, like the Oxford reformers, were men of the new school on the one hand, and opposed to the semi-pagan skepticism of the mere 'humanists' of Italy on the other hand. These men longed for reform, not only in morals but also in doctrine. They wanted

The mediating reformers of Italy. religion to be made a thing of the heart, that the gross superstition connected with indulgences and other abuses should be set aside, and some of them held the Augustinian doctrine of justification by faith. This gave them a sort of sympathy even with Luther, and they wanted such a reform of the Church as they hoped would win back the Protes-

Valdez, Pole, Contarini. tants into her fold. *Juan de Valdez*, brother of Charles V.'s secretary (from whose writings we have more than once quoted), was one of them. *Reginald Pole* (who opposed Henry VIII.'s revolt from Rome so strongly) and *Gaspar Contarini* (a Venetian nobleman of the highest character and influence in court circles) were of their number. They had among them eloquent preachers and ladies of rank, fortune, and beauty. They held together and exerted much influence, and there was a time when they seemed to be not without chance of success as mediators between the extreme Catholic and Protestant parties.

Paul III. became pope in 1534, and the hopes of the reform party were raised by his making Pole and Contarini and some others of their friends cardinals. These men were on the most friendly terms with Erasmus, who in his old age was urging concord on religious parties and purity on the Church. It was rumoured that Erasmus himself was to be made a cardinal, and it was said that a red hat was on the way to Bishop Fisher when he was executed by Henry VIII.

Paul III. makes some of them cardinals.

It was some of these and other signs of the times which cheered Sir Thomas More in his prison with the belief that better days were coming, that there was at least some chance of a reconciliation with the Protestants, and a healing of the schism by which the Church was rent. The prospect was for the moment promising. Paul III. wrote to Erasmus, telling him that he intended to call a council (as Erasmus had urged his predecessors to do) and asking for his influence and help both before and in the council. But things moved slowly. Cardinal Contarini was more zealous for a council than the Pope, who was only half-inclined to it, fearing lest it might abridge his power. At length in 1541—five years after the death of Erasmus—the Pope deputed

Chances of a reconciliation with Protestants under Paul III.

Contarini to meet the Protestants at the Diet
of Ratisbon, and to try whether a reconciliation could be arranged with them.   He was
met by the gentle Melanchthon (Luther dis-
trusting the whole thing and keeping away),
and they agreed upon the doctrine of justification by
faith as the basis of reunion.   For a moment a peace
seemed within reach.   But alas! other motives came in
on the Pope's side.   Francis I. urged upon
him that concord and unity in Germany
would make the Emperor—their common enemy—dan-
gerously strong ; and so Paul III. drew back.

(margin: Contarini and Melanchthon try to make peace at the Diet of Ratisbon.)

(margin: But the Pope draws back.)

On the other side, Luther scented mischief in any
peace with Rome.   It was too good to be
true ; and he even hinted that the devil was
somewhere and somehow at work in it.

(margin: And Luther also.)

So everything was left over for settlement
at the council which now at length the Pope
was to convene—the famous *Council of Trent*.
But meanwhile another power came upon the stage,
which was destined to take the reins out of the hands
of the Italian mediating reformers, to close the door for
reconciliation forever, and to reform what was left of the
Catholic Church on the narrow basis of reaction.

(margin: Everything left over till the Council of Trent.)

(b) *The New Order of the Society of Jesus* (1540).

Ignatius Loyola, a young Spanish knight of noble family, was born in 1491, and so was eight years younger
than Luther.   He was a soldier in the army
of Spain—that land in which the national
wars against the Moors had kept up chivalry
and the spirit of the old crusaders, in which knights still
fought for the Cross against the 'Infidel,' and whose citi-

(margin: Ignatius Loyola, a Spanish knight.)

zens more than any others felt the romance of the connexion with the New World.

Loyola was thirty years old, fighting in the Spanish
army against an insurrection in Navarre, secretly aided
by the French, just after the Diet of Worms,   He is wounded
when his leg was shattered by a cannon   in 1521
ball. The one hope of the young knight
was such a recovery as would let him return to his soldier's life and pursue his knightly career.   He submitted
to two cruel operations in this hope, but alas, in vain.
After racking torture and fever, which brought him near
to the grave, he survived to find his contracted limb still
a bar to his hopes.   As he lay upon his couch in pain
and fever, he changed the scheme of his   Resolves to be-
life. He resolved to become a soldier—a   come a general
general—in another army, under a higher   of an army of
king, fighting for the cross. Legends of the   of soldiers.
saints inspired his imagination with dreams still more
romantic than the tales of knight-errantry.   In his deli-
rium his fevered eye saw visions of the Virgin, and thus
he thought he received divine commission to pursue his
plan. He would be a true son of the Church, the sworn
enemy of her enemies, be they heretics, Jews, or infidels.
His creed should be the soldier's creed—obedience to
superiors, hard endurance, and dauntless courage.   The
holy saints of the legends were his patterns.   He prepared
himself for his work, as they did, by fastings and the se-
verest austerities.   His food was bread and water and
herbs, his girdle sometimes an iron chain,   His
sometimes prickly briars, his work humble   austerities.
service of the lowest kind, such as dressing
the foulest wounds in the hospitals.   Then he dwelt for
a while in a cavern in solitude, and fasted till he saw visions again, and fancied he had communications with

P

heaven.   And now he had perfected his plan—a soldier's plan—to found a religious army, perfect in discipline, in

Resolves to found the 'Order of Jesus.'

every soldier of which should be absolute devotion to one end, absolute obedience to his superior, with no human ties to hinder and no objects to divert him from the service required.   It was in fact to be a new monastic order, and to be called *the Society of Jesus.*

He must first prepare himself for his generalship by

To prepare himself studies at the University of Paris.

years of study.   He began at a common school, and then went to the University of Paris.

The next thing was to get round him a few others like himself, and so to form the nucleus of his army.   They must be men of power and metal, and all the better if of noble blood and high position.

There was a young Spanish noble at the university of

At Paris meets Francis Xavier.

Paris named Francis Xavier.   While Loyola was studying at the university he came in contact with him.   He watched him, read his mind and character, and then set himself to work to make his own.   Xavier sought fame and applause, and just as he got it, Loyola would come in his way with the solemn question, 'What shall it profit if a man gain the whole world and lose his own soul?'   Loyola would help him to new triumphs, but as often as they came would come to him again from Loyola the solemn question, 'What shall it profit?'.   At last the proud spirit of the Spanish noble yielded to the spell.   Xavier be-

Xavier becomes a disciple.

came a disciple of Loyola; rivalled him in austerities, and ere long became the missionary of the Society, carrying his cross, his Bible, breviary and wallet to India and the Indian Isles, and even to Japan and China, till at last he laid down

his life after eleven long years of heroic la- And the great
bour, stretched on the sand of the sea-shore Jesuit mission-
of a lonely island in the Chinese seas, with dies, China,
his cross in his hand, tears of holy joy in and Japan.
his eyes, and uttering the words, 'In Thee have I put
my trust, let me never be confounded.'

Of such stuff were the first Jesuits made—a type of
human nature which, rising up as it did just then, was
of immense import to the future of the Catholic Church.
It was in truth a reaction from the looseness both of
morals and creed which had marked the recent condition of the Church. These men were pious, Character of
earnest, and devoted to the Church, be- the Jesuits.
cause their minds were cast in a mould
which allowed them still to believe in her pretensions.
They had all the piety, fervour, energy, and boldness of
the Protestant Reformers, but their reform took another
direction. Instead of going back to St. Augustine as
their exponent of the Bible, they took St. Francis and
the mediæval saints as their models, and rested with absolute faith on the authority of the mediæval Church.
To reform the Catholic Church to mediæval standards
by the formation of a new monastic order, having for its
corner-stone the absolute surrender of free inquiry and
free thought, and absolute obedience to supreme ecclesiastical authority—this was the project of Their suc-
Loyola. It was not abortive. Before its cess and
founder died he had succeeded in founding influence.
more than a hundred Jesuit colleges or houses for train-
ing Jesuits, and an immense number of educational establishments under their influence. He had many thousands of Jesuits in the rank and file of his order. He
had divided Europe, India, Africa, and Brazil into twelve
Jesuit provinces, in each of which he had his Jesuit offi-

cer, whilst he, their general, residing at Rome, wielded
an influence over the world rivaling, if it did not exceed
in power, that of popes and kings. Its very success was
the cause of its ultimate doom. The nations of Europe,

Causes of its
ultimate
unpopularity.
after the experience of some generations,
found it to interfere with their national freedom, as they had done the old ecclesiastical
empire of Rome. They ultimately banished the Jesuits
because of their power and because their presence and
their plots endangered the safety of the state. But as
yet the Society of Jesus was young, and had its work
before it. The Order received Papal sanction in 1540.

(c) *The Council of Trent* (*1545—1555*).

The Council of Trent was opened in 1545. Cardinal
Contarini, who had been the Pope's confidant in matters

Council of
Trent meets
in 1545.
relating to the Council, died before it assembled. But Cardinal Pole, Contarini the
younger, and others of the mediating party,
were members of the Council. They took the same line
as at Ratisbon, and urged the doctrine of justification by
faith as common Christian ground. But the Jesuits in

The Jesuits
prevail over
the mediat-
ing Refor-
mers.
the Council, under the instruction of Loyola,
opposed it with all their might. The dispute
was long and hot, and even led to personal
violence. One holy Father was so angry
that he seized another by the beard. The Jesuits prevailed, and carried the decision of the Council their own
way. Pole, on the plea of ill health, had left the Council,
and the younger Contarini followed his example. It was
clear there was to be no reconciliation. The party of
reaction had gained the day.

No sooner had the party of reaction taken the lead
than Cardinal Caraffa (afterwards Pope Paul IV). ob-

tained powers to introduce into Rome the
Inquisition—that terrible tribunal of persecution which in Spain had slain and banished so many Moors, Jews, and heretics
under the sanction of the zeal of Queen Isabella.   Persecution began, and some of the members of
the mediating party were among its first victims.

Inquisition introduced into Rome by Cardinal Caraffa, afterwards Pope Paul IV.

This was the work of the Council of Trent at its early
sessions.   Then owing to a disagreement between the
Pope and Charles V., it was adjourned for
some years.   Paul III. died, and two succeeding popes, before it really got to work
again to any purpose under Paul IV.   This was in 1555,
the year in which, after the long struggle between
Charles V. and Germany, the peace of Augsburg was
come to, by which the revolt of the Protestant princes
from Rome was first legally recognized as a thing which
must be.

Council adjourned till 1555, under Paul IV.

The Council of Trent had now in its later sessions to
reorganize what was left of the Catholic Church.   It
could not, and did not try to undo the revolts.   The Jesuits were the ruling power.
Reaction was the order of the day.   Clerical abuses were corrected, and some sort of
decency enforced.   Provisions were made
for the education of priests and for their devotion in future to active duties.   But in points of doctrine there was reaction instead of concession.   The divine authority of the Pope was confirmed.   The creed
of the Church was laid down once for all in rigid statements, which henceforth must be swallowed by the faithful.   Finally, the Inquisition, imported from Spain, was
extended to other countries, and charged with the sup-
pression of heretical doctrines.   In a word, the rule of

The Roman Catholic Church reformed in morals, but much more rigid than ever in creed.

the ecclesiastical empire was strengthened, and the bonds of the scholastic system tightened; but not for Christendom—only for those nations who still acknowledged the ecclesiastical supremacy of Rome.

The Church was thus both reformed and narrowed by the decrees of the Council of Trent. Henceforth it tolerated within its fold neither the old diversity of doctrine on the one hand, nor the old laxity of morals on the other hand, and henceforth it was by no means coextensive with Western Christendom, as it once had been. It is now generally called the 'Roman Catholic Church,' to distinguish it from the 'Catholic Church' of the Middle Ages, from which it and so many other churches have sprung.

CHAPTER VI.

THE FUTURE OF SPAIN AND FRANCE.

(a) *The Future of Spain.*

CHARLES V. had inherited the absolute monarchy prepared for him by Ferdinand and Isabella.

The strengthening of the central power was needful to create a modern nation. But the history of England has taught us that the central power may be strong without being an absolute monarchy.

Growth of absolute monarchy in Spain. The vice in the Spanish system was the attempt to seek national power by subjecting all classes within the nation to the absolute will of the monarch.

This vice was the worm at the root of the greatness of Spain, and silently wrought the ruin in which she finds herself to-day.

Philip II. Philip II., the son and successor of Charles, was, like his predecessor, an absolute king.

It was during the period of Spanish supremacy in Europe that the Council of Trent decreed the absolute ecclesiastical supremacy of the Pope. It was the Spanish Jesuits who had brought this about. It was by adopting the Spanish Inquisition that the ecclesiastical triumph was to be enforced upon the people. And now Philip II.'s aim, as we have seen, was to establish both the absolute power of the Spanish throne and the papal supremacy, wherever his rule extended, by the sword and the Inquisition.

In close league with the Papacy.

Seeks to establish Spanish and Papal supremacy together.

England felt this influence in the days of Queen Mary, but happily Philip II.'s Spanish Armada failed to conquer England under Elizabeth. He tried his fatal policy in the Netherlands, and, as we have seen, they revolted, made good their revolt from both Spain and Rome, and became a free Protestant nation. He tried the same fatal policy in Spain, and with what result? The Spaniard of to-day points to the civil and ecclesiastical despotism of the reign of Philip II. (from which, unhappily, Spain could not shake herself free, as the Netherlands did) as the point in her history when her national life was strangled, her literature began to lose its power, her commerce to languish. To fatten an absolute monarchy, and armies of officials, soldiers, and priests, in course of generations the nation was ruined. Spain for a while was big on the map. For a while she maintained her supremacy in Europe, but her greatness was not the result of her advance on the path of modern civilization. It was not the result of true national life—the welding together of all classes into a compact nation. It rather belonged to the old order of things, and so was doomed to decay.

Fatal results of his policy.

(*b*) *The future of France.*

Absolute monarchy answered no better for France than for Spain.

France was a prey during the era to the evils caused by the constant wars of Francis I. While the two absolute monarchs strove for supremacy in Italy,

Everything sacrificed to gratify the ambition of the absolute monarchy under Francis I.

their subjects alike suffered. The recklessness of the ambition of Francis I. showed itself in the way in which, while persecuting heresy in France, he was ready to ally himself with the Protestants of Germany, or even the Turks, if need be, to gain his military ends. He bequeathed his ambition for military glory and supremacy to his successors.

France, though a Catholic power, fought on the Protestant side in the Thirty Years' War, and one result of it was that the supremacy of Spain ended and that of France began. But French, no less than Spanish supremacy, was the growth of absolute monarchy, contrary to the true interests of the French nation. It was gradually ripening the seeds which were already sown, and which bore fruit in the great Revolution of 1789, and in the alternate republics and despotisms under

The curse which her absolute monarchy was to France.

which France has since suffered so much. The want of common feeling and interest between the citizens of the towns and peasants of the rural districts which began so early in French history still continues to perplex her rulers, and so does the lust for military glory and supremacy in Europe which also is an old inheritance of the French people.

The way in which the Protestant revolution was met in France also left scars upon the nation which may be traced to-day. Under Francis I., Calvinism spread in

France among the nobility, whose order had been humbled to make way for the absolute mon- archy. This gave rise in the next era to religious wars, in which some of the Protestant nobility headed a rebellion against the Catholic throne. These civil wars lasted forty years, and cost the lives, it is said, of more than a million Frenchmen.

In France the persecution of heresy was political as well as religious. Political ambition and intrigue, as well as religious bigotry, prompted it, and stained the pages of French history with crimes unique in their blackness.

The massacre of St. Bartholomew in 1572 was the diabolical work of the queen, Catherine de' Medici, to maintain her political power. She had coquetted with the Huguenots when it served her purpose. She tried to exterminate them by the massacre of 20,000—some say 100,000—in one fatal night. The Edict of Nantes in 1598 ended the civil wars and granted a respite from persecution, but its revocation in 1685 resulted in the banishment of the Huguenots from France. Some of them came to Protestant England, and brought with them their silk and their looms. Thus France by her intolerance lost one arm of her national industry and an important element from her national character. The want of cohesion and unity of interest between various classes in France was increased by the banishment of the Huguenots. There is even now a middle term wanting—a missing link—between her religious and her republican elements. The Puritans—the religious republicans— were that middle term in England.

CHAPTER VII.

GENERAL RESULTS OF THE ERA OF THE PROTESTANT
REVOLUTION.

(*a*) *On the Growth of National Life.*

WE have now traced the course of the Protestant revo-

Influence of the Protestant revolution on national life. lution, and marked both its direct results upon those nations which revolted from Rome, and also its indirect results upon Rome herself and those nations which remained in allegiance to her ecclesiastical empire.

The revolution was obviously only partially success-

Where it succeeded. ful. Where it succeeded it produced reform—the Protestant nations had gained one substantial step towards independent national life and towards the blending of all classes within them into one community.

Where it failed, it produced, as every unsuccessful

Where it failed. revolution does, *reaction*. The Catholic nations seemed to gain in the outward signs of strength by the alliance which resulted between the civil and ecclesiastical powers within them. But it was an alliance intended to strengthen the absolute power of the Crown and of the ecclesiastical empire, and thereby all the more to enthrall the people. Henceforth, both in France and in Spain, the nation was more than ever enthralled under the double despotism of Crown and Church. The Inquisition may be taken as the symbol of the one kind of despotism, and the French Bastille of the other. The two despotisms acting together tended, as we have seen, to destroy national life, to increase the separation of classes and prevent their being welded together by common interests into one community. It postponed their progress on the path of modern civilization and ended in a series of alternate revolutions and reactions, out of which it is hard to see a final escape. So hard is it for nations to cast off the fruit, however bitter, of seeds sown even centuries ago!

Where it partially failed and partially succeeded, as in Switzerland and Germany, we have seen that it resulted in civil wars and in the postponement of the growth of their national life almost to our own times. In Switzerland the people were already free, but in Germany, where serfdom still prevailed, the emancipation of the peasantry was postponed till the beginning of the nineteenth century.

Where it partly failed and partly succeeded.

(b) *On the Relations of Nations to each other.*

The Protestant struggle apparently did little or nothing to secure progress in civilization in the dealings between nations. The events of the era show that the notion of universal empire which had marked the old order of things was not yet fully given up. The aim after extension of empire which went along with it we have noticed throughout. The struggle between the two absolute monarchies of Spain and France for supremacy in Christendom, the efforts of the princes of the House of Hapsburg to unite as many countries as they could under their rule, the designs that both France and Spain had upon Italy, the revived claims of Henry VIII. to the old English possessions in France—in all this there was little sign of progress from the old to the new order of things. Although the Oxford reformers were faithful in enjoining upon princes an international policy based upon the golden rule, and having for its object not the aggrandizement of the prince

Small improvement in the dealings between nations.

The Oxford reformers not listened to in this.

but the weal of the nation, the popes and princes still preferred to follow the maxims of *"the Prince"* of Machiavelli, rather than those of the *" Christian Prince"* of Erasmus. They still, as Erasmus said, treated the people too much as " cattle in the market."

Nor was the immediate result of the Protestant revolution any cessation from international strife. For the next hundred years there was almost incessant strife between Catholic and Protestant powers.

Though, however, Henry VIII. himself hankered again and again after the realization of the empty title of King of France; yet practically we may say that Henry VIII.'s dreams were the last in which English monarchs have indulged on that subject.

But Henry VIII. was the last English king to dream of recovering France.

And though the attempts to urge sounder views on international matters did not succeed in this era, yet they were not made wholly in vain. Before the century was out was born *Hugo Grotius*, the father of the present system of international law, who was well acquainted with the works of Erasmus, and like him rejected Machiavellian principles and sought to base the law of nations upon the golden rule.

And *Hugo Grotius* was born before the century was out.

(c) *Influence on the Growth of National Languages and Literature.*

In no point was the effect of the Protestant struggle more clearly marked than in the stride it gave, as it were all at once, to the growth of national languages and literature.

In Germany we noticed how Luther and Hutten appealed to the people as well as to the learned; how, first writing in Latin for scholars, they soon found it needful to write in German for the people; how Luther introduced wood-cuts to make his appeals to the popular ear still more vivid and telling. All this promoted the growth of a national popular literature. This turning from Latin to German was in fact throwing off in one point the yoke of the scholastic system, and was in itself a great step in advance for the nation to have taken. The crowning gift of Luther to the German people was in fact his German Bible and his German hymns. The earnest vigorous German in which they are written fixed the future style of the language. The German spoken to-day is the German of Luther's Bible and hymns. They have been better known by the German people than any other literature, and so have done more than perhaps anything else to form the German language, and with it in no small degree the national character.

Luther's Bible and hymns fix the character of the German language.

It was so in some measure in France. Calvin did not gain so great a hold on the French nation as Luther did on the German, but still his French Writings did very much the same thing for the French language that Luther's Bible did for the German.

Influence of Calvin's writings on the French language.

In England, too, the same thing is to be marked. The fact that the religious controversies of the times were carried on by books and pamphlets, not in Latin but in English, gave a stimulus to English literature, and prepared the way for the succeeding generations which were to give England her Shakespeare and her Milton. Nor can it be forgotten that the noble English version of the Bible has done as much as other versions in other countries to fix the character of mo

Influence of Tindal's New Testament on the English version of the Bible, and so upon the English language.

dern English.   The simplicity, terseness, and power of
the English version, to which the taste of England, after
frequent wanderings, again and again returns as to its
best classical model, we owe, and this should not be
forgotten, to the poor, persecuted, but noble-minded
English reformer, William Tindal, who, in his English
New Testament, set a type which others in completing
the translation of the whole Bible loyally followed.

(*d*) *Effect in Stimulating National Education.*

The same movement which promoted so much the
growth of national language and literature, also did much
to throw open the gates of knowledge to the people by
fostering education and schools.

Savonarola founded schools in Florence.   Colet set a
noble example in England, and the next generation followed it by establishing the grammar-schools
which so often bear the name of King Edward VI.   Luther and the Protestant German states established common schools.
Calvin did the same thing in Geneva, and
Calvin's disciple, John Knox, in Scotland.
Finally, the Pilgrim Fathers carried the same
zeal for education to their colonies in New England.
Even the Jesuits made a great point of education, and
became noted wherever they went for their educational
establishments.   So that both in Catholic and Protestant
countries a great stimulus was given to popular education
during the era, while the fact that at least some of the
property of the dissolved monasteries was diverted to
educational purposes in connexion with the Universities
and otherwise, gave a somewhat similar stimulus also to
higher education.

*[Marginal note: Schools found-
ed by Savona-
rola, Colet. and
others, Luther,
Calvin, Knox,
the Pilgrim
Fathers, and
the
Jesuits.]*

(*e*) *Influence on Domestic Life.*

There are few things, if any, more important to the steady growth of a free nation than the maintenance of domestic virtues and the sanctities of family life.

The domestic instincts, more than any others, were the first germs of national life. In Teutonic nations especially the powerful ties of family life, widening in their sphere extended from the family to the tribe, from the tribe to the nation, introducing law and order and peaceful relations within the sphere embraced by them.

Political importance of domestic life.

Now the domestic virtues of nations had been in great danger of decay, and no doubt had suffered enormously through the influence of so large a body of clergy, monks, and nuns in a forced state of celibacy.

Danger to it from the existence in a country of large celibate classes.

This system sapped the foundations of domestic life by holding up the married state as lower in virtue than that of celibacy, by cutting off so large a number of people from the natural influences of home-life, and still further by promoting in a terrible degree immorality and crime.

The dissolution of the monasteries and permission of the marriage of the parochial clergy were in themselves steps gained in civilization of great importance in a moral and political, as well as in a religious point of view.

Dissolution of monasteries and permission to the clergy to marry, a step in civilization.

(*f*) *Influence on Popular Religion.*

In yet another way did the Protestant revolution succeed in promoting national life and the aims of Christian civilization.

It made religion less a thing of the clergy and more a thing of the people. It gave the people religious ser-

The Protes-
tant move-
ment popu-
larized re-
ligion,

vices in their own languages instead of in an unknown tongue. By placing within their reach the Christian Scriptures in their own language it led them to think for them-selves, and to be directly influenced by Christianity as taught by its founder and apostles. It tended to strengthen individual conviction and conscience, and so ultimately it led, though with many drawbacks, to fur-ther steps being gained towards freedom of thought.

It is well to mark also that this bringing of religion nearer home to the individual conscience of the masses

and brought
it into har-
mony with
true Chris-
tianity and
modern
civilization.

of the people, and cultivation of individual responsibility rather than reliance on a priesthood or a church, tended to bring it more into harmony, not only with the ten-dencies of modern civilization but also with the essential character of Christianity itself, as conceived by its founder and his apostles, and so to make it once more the great civilizing influence which from the first it was intended to be.

Christianity was without doubt the power which more than anything else produced the great movement of the

Modern
civilization
owes its
chief charac-
teristic to
Christianity.

era, and turned the civilization of the future into the course we have described. The mere humanists had not succeeded in im-pressing the semi-pagan stamp of their phi-losophy upon it. Had they done so the principle of the old Roman civilization—the good of the few at the expense of the many—might have marked the civilization of the future as it had done that of the past. But we have seen it was the men of deepest Christian convictions—the religious reformers—who succeeded in giving their impress to the era. It is thus to Christianity more than to anything else that we owe the direction given in the era to modern civilization, its characteristic aim to attain the highest good for the whole community.

(g) *Want of Progress in Toleration.*

There was one thing especially in which there seemed to be reaction rather than progress during the era, viz. in toleration.

We said that one great work of the era was to set men's minds free from ecclesiastical and scholastic thraldom—to set both science and religion free, for without this freedom there could be no real progress in civilization.

In fact, an immense number of minds had got free from that particular ecclesiastical and scholastic thraldom against which they had rebelled in becoming . Protestant. And this in itself was no small result. But what has already been said must have made it clear that the Protestant reformers, in adopting the theology of St. Augustine, and insisting upon their followers adopting the new Protestant creeds, did but appeal from the scholastic standards of their day to others just as rigid.

Change from Catholic to Protestant creeds was change from one rigid scholastic creed to another equally rigid.

The Oxford Reformers had aimed at leaving people open to form their own honest judgment on various points of theology and practice, according to their own consciences, and urged that people with different opinions and practice might be members of the same Christian Church, have charity one towards another, and agree to differ without quarrelling. But how hard a

Small connexion between claiming freedom of thought and conceding it to others.

Q

thing it was to get people to do this we see from the case
of Sir Thomas More himself, who, though he had advo-
cated toleration in his 'Utopia,' yet afterwards, seeing
the anarchy Protestantism had led to on the Continent,
and fearing its spreading to England, became himself a
persecutor. We must not be surprised after this that the
Protestant Reformers failed also in the same respect. It
is strange to see how little connexion there seems to be
between claiming freedom of thought and conceding it
to others.

Lutherans persecuted Catholics as well as Catholics
Protestants; and, worse still, they persecuted their fel-
low-Protestants who followed Zwingle and Calvin rather
than Luther. So Calvin put Servetus to death, and ex-
So persecution
did not make
the persecuted
tolerant. ercised a thoroughly intolerant rule in
Geneva. So the English Government, after
the revolt from Rome, persecuted Protes-
tants, and soon after ordered by statute practices which
a few years before they had condemned. So the Catholic Government of Queen Mary shed the blood of Protestants again. So the English Protestant Church of
after generations persecuted the Puritans. So finally,
the Puritans, fleeing from persecution to New England,
put people to death for no other crime than that they
honestly preached doctrines differing from their own!
Looking at these facts, one would certainly say that the
Protestant struggle had not made men more tolerant!

And yet, in spite of this temporary failure, toleration
was a distant fruit of the great movement we have
Yet toleration
was after all
one of the ulti-
mate results of
the Protestant
revolution. traced. In this era its first seeds were
sown. Sir Thomas More's 'Utopia' was
perhaps the first clear statement of the doctrine of toleration. The works of Erasmus
did something, probably more than is

known, to prepare the minds of men for its ultimate adoption. The strength of conscientious conviction which Protestantism created made men claim freedom as a right, and after all, the men who were fighting the battle of toleration with most effect, were the men whose strength of conscientious conviction made them endure persecution rather than surrender their freedom of conscience, even though they themselves, under other circumstances, might have been persecutors.

(h) *The Causes why the Success of the Era was so partial.*

We might, in view simply of its immediate results—the wars and bloodshed, and anarchy, persecutions, and heartburnings which came out of it—be inclined to regard the failures of the era of the Protestant revolution as greater than the good we owe to it.

This would be false. It would be to forget that progress in civilization is of necessity like that of the advancing tide, made up of ebbs and flows. It is well also to note clearly the cause of the failures, and especially of those of which we have just been speaking.

Progress must be gradual.

Let us ask ourselves why did not the human mind in this era free itself from its trammels, claim its true freedom, and concede it to everyone? The answer is, that it was impossible. The range of knowledge was too narrow. Men's minds could not take a broader view of things than the horizon of their knowledge let them.

Limited by the range of men's knowledge.

Let us try to realize what were the bounds of their knowledge in some directions.

They knew that the earth is a globe, and in their own time Magellan, for the first time, had sailed round it.

Limited view of the universe.

But they thought the earth was in the centre of the universe, and that all the heavenly bodies move round it every twenty-four hours. The notion that it was the earth that moved they thought to be absurd. We should *see* the motion, they said. At the rate it would have to move, it would leave the clouds behind it as it went, and towers and church steeples would be thrown down by the violence of so rapid a motion!

The earth still thought to be in the centre.

So the earth stands still, they maintained in the centre of the universe. The heavenly bodies were supposed to rotate on what were called *crystalline spheres*. The first was the sphere of the moon—all things confined within it were called *sublunary* things. They were supposed by some to be under such pressure as made the heaviest things all tend towards the centre, while the lightest things tended upwards. It was sometimes said that it was in the nature of fire and air to rise, while it was the nature of water and earth to fall towards the centre. In rough ways like these they tried to account for the facts which are now attributed to the force of gravitation. The spheres beyond the moon were called *celestial* spheres. First, they thought, came those of Mercury, Venus, and the Sun, then in order those of Mars, Jupiter, and Saturn; then that of the fixed stars, and, outside all, a ninth sphere, called *primum mobile*, which gave motion to all the others. They believed further, in a vague way, that heaven came beyond. Theologians speculated upon what sort of a sphere that of heaven must be, and Erasmus, in his 'Praise of Folly,' laughed at their 'creating new spheres at pleasure, this the largest and most beautiful being added that, forsooth, happy spirits

The crystalline spheres.

Heaven beyond.

might have room enough to take a walk, to spread their feasts, or play at ball.'

Such was the universe of spheres, one within the other, which they thought all moved round the earth in the centre every twenty-four hours. It was a small thing altogether, compared with the vastly wider and grander universe, a little bit of which modern science has revealed to us, but it was a marvellous universe still, and its mysteries filled them with awe when they thought of it.

The motions of the spheres regarded with awe,

When asked questions about it, some wise men like Erasmus answered, ' God only knows.' But more superstitious minds gave far different answers. Luther, who saw the action of the Devil in every accident which befell him, stood aghast at the magic motions of the celestial spheres, as ' no doubt done by some angel.' Many wise men still believed in astrology. They could not bring themselves to believe that the stars and planets, looking down upon our world, had not some magic meaning. When comets came, they saw in them ominous presages of coming events. Pico and Ficino, Colet, Erasmus, and More had all tried to laugh people out of belief in astrology. Luther, too, laughed at it, but Melanchthon still held on to the old belief in spite of Luther's arguments and jests. How can there be anything in astrology, Luther used to say to him, since Jacob and Esau were born under the same star !

and in popular superstition referred to angels.

Astrology.

Laughed at by some, but believed in by others.

The same kind of superstition which attributed the motions of the planets to angels, and magic influence on the affairs of men to the stars, made men the more readily believe in visions and inspirations, such as we have seen in the case

Belief in visions and inspirations.

·of the wilder reformers from Savonarola down to Münzer and Loyola.   Luther himself was remarkably free
from these things—he never claimed either visions or inspirations, as the wilder prophets did ; but, as an instance of how superstitious even he was, it may be mentioned that he and Melanchthon devoutly believed that
and in prodi-   a monster had been found in the Tiber, with
gies.   the head of an ass, the body of a man, and
the claws of a bird.   After searching their Bibles to find
out what the prodigy meant, they concluded that it was
one of the signs and wonders which were to precede
the fall of the papacy, and published a pamphlet about
it.

Luther again, and probably everybody else, believed
in witchcraft.   Hundreds and thousands of poor wretches
Universal   were burned for the supposed crime of hav-
belief in   ing sold themselves to the powers of evil,
witchcraft.   and having held communion with evil
spirits.   And stranger still is it that the number of witches
Witches as   burned was rapidly on the increase.   There
well as here-   were more witches burned in the 16th cen-
tics burned.   tury than in any previous one, and more
still in the next.

Heresy and witchcraft were looked upon as nearly
allied, and probably the zeal against both grew together.
Nor was the cruel death allotted to these supposed crimes
out of proportion to that of others.   Thousands and
thousands of people were hung in England for no other
crime but that of vagrancy and ' sturdy begging.'   The
Cruelty of   system of criminal law was everywhere
criminal law   brutal.   Soon after the Peasants' War, the
everywhere.   Prince Bishop of Bamberg published a
popular criminal law book for the benefit of his subjects
—his poor crushed peasantry among others—in which

were inserted wood-cuts of thumb-screws, the rack, the
gallows, the stake, pincers for pulling out the tongue,
men with their eyes put out or their heads cut off, or
mangled on the wheel, or suspended by the arms with
weights hung on their feet, and so on, and then, to add
the terrors of another world (as if these humanly inflicted tortures were not enough), there was a blasphe-
mous picture representing the day of judgment, and the
hobgoblins carrying off their victims to hell. The Prince
Bishop, we may suppose, had learned a lesson from
Luther, and produced, as he thought, a *good book for
the laity*, meant, not like Luther's, to dispel men's fears
of the Pope, but to frighten his poor subjects into submission to his episcopal and princely authority. This
may be taken as an example both of the way in which
civil and ecclesiastical power were sometimes blended
together, and of the brutality of the times.

Such an age was not ready for wider views. Further
knowledge of the laws of nature must come   The age not
before popular superstitions could be re-   prepared for
moved, and until this was done it would be   toleration.
in vain to look for much progress in toleration and freedom of thought.

(*i*) *Beginning of Progress in Scientific Inquiry.*

Nevertheless the era of which we have spoken was
the beginning of the era of freedom. From it dated a
great awaking of human thought. Its great   Beginning of
geographical discoverers had opened new   scientific in-
fields for scientific inquiry. Not only had   quiry.
navigators been round the world, but they had seen as
it were the rest of the sky. They had seen the south
polestar and the Southern Cross in their voyages round
the Cape of Good Hope. Thus was not only their

geographical but also their astronomical knowledge widened.

A beginning of truer and wider views of the universe was almost a natural consequence, but to attain to it scholastic and even ecclesiastical bonds had to be loosened. A scientific Luther was wanted to burst through them, but the age did not produce such a man. Nevertheless it did produce one who silently lived and worked timidly to demonstrate that the motions of the planets and the moon can only be fully accounted for on the hypothesis that the sun and not the earth is the centre of the solar system, that the moon is a satellite of the earth, and that the sphere of the fixed stars is at an immense distance from the farthest of the planetary spheres. Our present theory of the solar system is still sometimes called after his name, *Copernican*, though it is far more truly called after Newton.

Nicolas Copernicus died two years before Luther. His story is that of a brave life, and one which may well be set by the side of that of other great men of the era. Educated at the University of Cracow, in Poland, he afterwards proceeded to Rome, and studied under the best astronomer of the day. Then he spent a long life in working out his grand scientific problem from careful observations and according to the best lights he could get. He was loyal to the Church. He did not want to be a heretic, and yet the great truth he had to tell was contrary to the teaching of the Church. For thirty-six years—all the time the Protestant struggle was raging—he was working at the immortal book in which his observations and discoveries were embodied, but he did not venture to publish it till under Paul III. there was a lull in the ecclesiastical storm. He was then an old man,

Nicolas Copernicus.

in broken health; his book was in the printer's hands when he was on his death-bed. All he cared for now was to see it safe in print before he died. He waited at death's door day after day. At last the printer's messenger came with the printed book. He received it with tears in his eyes, composed himself and died. This was in 1543, and he was seventy years old. He was followed by other scientific discoverers—Tycho Brahe, Kepler, and Galileo. Thus the brave life of Copernicus may be taken as marking the epoch when scientific thought and inquiry began to free itself from theological trammels and to seek to discover the laws of nature by a simple, childlike, and careful observation of facts. But necessarily many generations must pass away before men became used to scientific modes of research and of thought.

His great work not published till he was on his death-bed.

CHAPTER VIII.

ECONOMIC RESULTS OF THE ERA.

AMONGST the powers which belonged to the old order of things, and which were going out, the feudal system was mentioned as silently giving way under the combined influence of the growth of the central power in the modern nations and of commerce.

Results of the era on what remained of the feudal system.

The results of the era in hastening the dissolution of the feudal system require a few words of further explanation.

In Germany, we have seen, serfdom—the essential of which, it will be remembered, was services of forced

In Germany personal services continued.

personal labor in return for occupation of land—remained unchanged, except for the worse, after the Peasants' War, and lasted on till the beginning of the present century.

In France serfdom was a thing of the past, but there
In France feudal rents and payments chiefly *in kind* continued till 1798.
remained numberless feudal rents and payments made *chiefly in kind* (*i. e.* in produce of the land) which the peasantry went on paying till the French Revolution of 1798.

In England serfdom was gone, but had left behind it *fixed rents in money* instead of the old feudal payments
In England feudal rents were chiefly in fixed money payments.
in services or in kind. These rents were originally nearly equal to the annual value of the land. But an economic cause came into play during the era which, while it did
not help the German peasant nor the French peasant who
Effect of the discovery of the silver mines in the New World.
paid his rent in kind, lessened the burden of the English peasant's rent so much as to change his position gradually into that of an absolute owner.

This economic cause was the discovery of the silver and gold mines in the New World.

It made silver more plentiful, and therefore cheaper in proportion to other things, such as corn and land. In other words, it increased the price in pence and shillings
The fall in the value of money caused a great rise in prices.
of almost everything. A penny or a shilling would not buy so much corn after as before the new mines were discovered; and as in England Tudor monarchs at the same time for their own purposes, lessened the weight of silver in the penny and shilling by about one-third, the effect of the increased plenty of silver was made all the greater; 6s. would buy a quarter of wheat at the beginning of the

century, it took 38s. 6d. to buy a quarter of wheat at the end of it. The annual value of land was about 4d. per acre at the beginning of the century, 30d. at the end of it.

The German peasant was not helped by this, for he had to work just as many hours a day for his feudal landlord at the end as at the beginning of the century. *This did not lessen the German peasant's services.*

The French peasant, so far as he paid in produce, was not helped by it, because the price of his produce had increased as fast as the value of the land, and his rent remained the same burden as before. *Nor the French peasant's rents in produce.*

But the English peasant, who in the year 1500 paid 4d. an acre fixed rent for his land, which was then worth about 4d. an acre in the market, found himself in 1600, if he still held on to his land, still paying only 4d. an acre, while his land was worth in the market six, seven, or eight times as much as that. His burden of rent was reduced to ⅛th or ⅛th of what it used to be. *But it reduced the burden of the English peasants' rents in money to ⅙th or ⅛th of the value of their land. This would have made them peasant proprietors had they held on to their land. But their*

Had the English peasantry held on to their land as the German and French peasants did, they would thus have grown into peasant proprietors, paying very small nominal rents for their land. But other economic causes were at work, tending to loosen them *tendency was to leave their land and become labourers for wages.* from their little holdings and make them labourers for wages. The growth of commerce and manufactures attracted them to the towns, the large farms of men with capital more and more took the place of the little peasant holdings, and thus began the present state of things in which England differs so much from other countries.

There were perhaps, in the year 1500, about half a

million families in England living by the land, and most

Change from
peasant pro-
prietorship
of land or
of looms to
labour for
wages,
were, or had been, farming some little bit of
land for themselves. Perhaps there were not
so many as a quarter of a million families
earning their living by trade or manufactures
in the towns, and most of them owning their
own workshops or looms.

The half million agricultural families have now grown
into about a million. These no longer are occupiers of
land, but are mostly working for wages for a few hundred thousand farmers. But in the meantime the two
or three hundred thousand families living by trade and
manufactures have increased to 3,000,000, and these
again, as a general rule, like their agricultural brethren,
have become workers for wages, and no longer are
owners of their own workshops and looms.

We probably owe this to the growth of capital and
commercial enterprise, stimulated by the increased profit

chiefly the
result of the
growth of
commerce
and capital,
and the use
of machinery.
which comes from division of labour, and
doing things on a large scale by machinery
rather than on a small scale as of old by
hand labour. But what we have to mark
here is that the beginnings of these great
changes were already at work in the era of
which we have been speaking, and that in their course
the last remains of the old feudal system have been demo-
lished in England. We only see in England now traces

These changes
had begun
in the 16th
century, and
they com-
pleted the-
silent down-
fall of the
feudal system
in England.
of a sort of mock-feudalism in the deer
forests and game preserves, and antiquated
forms and customs still clinging to the laws
of land tenure. These things are survivals
of a system which once had life, but which
belonged to the old order of things. In the
16th century it was already fast dying out

to make way for commercial enterprise and all that belongs to the new order of things—an order of things which has multiplied by six or seven the population of England, and peopled with about an equal additional number of Englishmen those great colonies for which the maritime enterprise of the 16th century first opened the way.

CONCLUSION.

In the introductory chapter we said that the passage from the old decaying form of civilization to the new, better, and stronger one, involved a change which must needs take place slowly and by degrees; but that in the era under review was to be the *crisis* of the change—the final struggle between the two forces.

We have now traced the main lines of the history of this crisis, and tried to point out its connexion with the future as well as with the past. We have seen that the Protestant revolution was but one wave of the advancing tide of modern civilization. It was a great *revolutionary* wave, the onward swell of which, beginning with the refusal of reform at the Diet of Worms, produced the Peasants' War and the Sack of Rome, swept on through the revolt of the Netherlands, the Thirty Years' War, the Puritan Revolution in England under Oliver Cromwell, the formation of the great independent American republic, until it came to a head and broke in all the terrors of the French Revolution.

The Protestant revolution was the beginning of a great revolutionary wave which broke in the French Revolution of 1798.

It is impossible not to see in the course of the events of this remarkable period an onward movement as

The movement was inevitable, and might have been peacefully met and aided by timely reforms.

irresistible and certain in its ultimate progress as that of the geological changes which have passed over the physical world.

It is in vain to speculate upon what might have been the result of the concession of broad measures of reform everywhere (as in England) whilst yet there was time; but in view of the bloodshed and misery which, humanly speaking, might have been spared, who can fail to be impressed with the terrible responsibility, in the eye of history, resting upon those by whom in the 16th century, at the time of the crisis, the reform was refused? They were utterly powerless, indeed, to stop the ultimate flow of the tide, but they had the terrible power to turn, what might otherwise have been a steady and peaceful stream, into a turbulent and devastating flood. They had the terrible power, and they used it, to involve their own and ten succeeding generations in the turmoils of revolution.

But the refusal of reform at the time of the crisis involved ten generations in the turmoils of revolution.

NOTES ON BOOKS IN ENGLISH RELATING
TO THE REFORMATION.

THE term "Reformation" is used by historical writers in two meanings. It quite frequently denotes the religious movement, which began under the auspices of Luther, Calvin, Cranmer and other leaders, and involved an emancipation from the rule of the Papacy, and an important change in the interpretation of the Gospel, as well as in the rites of Christian worship. The Reformation, as thus regarded, is an exclusively religious and ecclesiastical revolution. As such, it forms a portion of the history of Christianity and the Church. At the same time, Protestantism, as a religious system, was partly dependent for its origin on circumstances which properly fall within the province of secular history; and the progress of Protestantism, and of the conflict with the Papacy, is inextricably connected with the general course of European affairs. Hence, the general condition of society at the opening of the sixteenth century, the causes other than religious which prepared for the outbreaking of the great Protest against Rome, and the events of political history which link themselves to the religious Reform, must fall under the notice of a historian who takes a comprehensive view of his subject.

But the term "Reformation" is frequently used with more latitude as a convenient designation for the opening era of modern history,—the history of the post-mediæval times. While the religious reform was one leading and defining characteristic of the new era, it was not the sole peculiarity that distinguished it. On the contrary, various and complex elements, appear in the modern as distinguished from the mediæval period. Events like the growth of monarchy, the spread of Commerce, the new birth of Art, the Revival of Learning, are essential features in that form of society which gradually arose, and followed upon the Middle Ages. The historian who undertakes to describe the era as a whole must give its proper place to each of these new elements. He must trace each to its sources, and form an estimate of the reciprocal influence and collective effect of each of these features of society as it emerged from the mediæval condition. But he will, under such a plan, still be obliged to give a central place to the religious movement, both in the centuries which preceded Luther, and in the age contemporaneous with him. The Protestant religion cannot be considered as an incident; it must be treated as a vital, as the most commanding, fact in the new epoch. So that whether the Reformation is taken in the more special sense to which we first adverted, or in the more comprehensive meaning, the same facts come under the survey of the historian. The difference is chiefly in the point of view from which these facts are regarded, which will of course determine their grouping. As regards the mediæval period, secular history and ecclesiastical history are inseparable. Neither can be studied apart from the other. If a division is more possible as relates to the modern era, still even here, one class of phenomena are so closely associated with another, that ecclesiastical history cannot be understood apart from secular, nor can secular history be adequately studied apart from ecclesiastical. The life of nations, as of men, is one.

In the following list of some of the most useful works to be found in English on the Reformation, general literary works, as well as distinctively ecclesiastical writers, are included.

I. *The Period before Luther.* On Wickliffe, the Reforming Councils, and the beginnings of the Revival of Learning, the last two (viith and viiith) volumes of Milman's *Latin Christianity* are valuable. The fifth volume of the same work describes the Waldenses and other sects, of an earlier - date. Ullmann's *Reformers before the Reformation* (2 vols., Edinburgh, 1855) gives an excellent account of the theological and religious forerunners of Luther, especially in Germany. Gillett's *Life and Times of John Huss* (2 vols., 1871) is a readable narrative of the career of the Bohemian Reformer. Villari's *Life of Savonarola* is a thorough biography (2 vols., 1873). With it may be read George Eliot's (Mrs. Lewes's) *Romola*. The most recent *Life of Erasmus* is by Drummond (2 vols., 1873). Milman's Article on Erasmus (*Quart. Rev.*, No. ccxi., and in his collected *Essays*) is an elaborate and instructive discussion. Jortin's *Life of Erasmus* is a learned, but at the same time, an interesting biography, abounding in extracts from the writings of Erasmus. Upon Erasmus and his associates, the friends of the New Learning, in England, we have Seebohm's *The Oxford Reformers of 1498* (London, 1869). The literature of the age prior to Luther is described in the work of Hallam, *Introduction to the Lit. of Europe in the 15th, 16th, and 17th centuries* (3 vols., 1855-56).

II. *General Works upon the Reformation.* Robertson's *History of Charles V.* Edited by W. H. Prescott, with supplement on the Cloister Life of the Emperor (3 vols., 1856). Robertson prefixes to his work an Essay

on the state of Europe at the accession of Charles.
Prescott's *History of the Reign of Ferdinand and Isabella*, exhibits the causes which gave its peculiar tone to
Spanish Catholicism, prior to the sixteenth century.
Ranke, *History of the Popes of Rome during the sixteenth and seventeenth centuries.* Translated by Sarah
Austin, (3 vols., 1867). This is a work of the highest
value. Häusser, *The Period of the Reformation*, 1517-
1648. Translated from the German by Mrs. G. Sturges
(New York, 1874) is a very able series of historical lectures, and is especially valuable for the political side of
the history of this period. Guizot's *Lectures on the History of Civilization* contain two chapters on the Reformation and its consequences. D'Aubigné's *History
of the Reformation* is a full, detailed narrative, in a viva-
cious style, by a warm advocate of Protestantism. On
the Catholic side is Spaulding's *History of the Reformation* (Baltimore, 1866). Balmes, *Protestantism and Cath-
olicity compared in their effects on Civilization :* translated from the Spanish (1851), is a voluminous polemi-
cal book, by a Spanish Priest, in reply to Guizot's
Lectures on Civilization. *The Reformation*, by G. P.
Fisher, is designed "to present to intelligent and educated readers the means of acquainting themselves "
with the Reformation, in its various aspects (1 vol.,
1873).

The ivth vol. of Gieseler's *Church History* (in the
American Edition) is an extremely learned and satisfac-
tory account of the Reformation; but it is adapted to
scholars, and not to the general reader. Hardwick's
History of the Reformation is likewise intended for
scholars and theologians, and is written by a decided
adherent of the Church of England. The chapters on
the Reformation in Hase's *Church History* are less

scholastic, but are still specially adapted to the theologi‑ cal scholar. Waddington's *History of the Reformation,* is a carefully written, impartial narrative, of a more popular character ; but it extends only to the death of Luther.

III. *Works upon the Reformation in the several coun‑ tries.* (*a*) *Germany.* At the head of the list belongs Ranke's *History of Germany in the Period of the Re‑ formation :* translated in part, by Sarah Austin, (3 vols., 1845-47). Michelet's *Life of Luther* (1 vol.), and *Table-Talk of Luther,* are both translated in Bohn's Library. The *Life of Luther* by Barnas Sears (8 vo., 1850), is brief, but founded on an extensive knowledge of the sources.

(*b*) *Switzerland.* Christoffel's *Zwingli, or the Rise of the Reformation in Switzerland,* is one of the latest biographies of the Zurich Reformer. The *Life of Cal‑ vin,* by Beza, translated from the Latin by Gibson (Philad., 1836), is one of the original documents relating to the subject. The *Life of Calvin* by Dyer (1849) is accurate and impartial. The most copious and com‑ plete of the biographies of Calvin is by Henry, trans‑ lated from the German by Stebbing (3 vols., 1844). *The Letters of Calvin,* edited by Bonnet, translated in 2 vols. (Edinburgh, 1856-57), are important. There is an English translation of all of Calvin's Writings, in 52 vols. (Edinburgh, 1856-57).

(*c*) *Denmark, Norway, and Sweden.* Dunham, *His‑ tory* of these countries (in Lardner's Cab. Cycl., 1840). Geijer, *History of Sweden,* translated by Turner (1845).

(*d*) *Bohemia and Moravia. The Reformation and Anti-Reformation in Bohemia* (2 vols., London, 1845.)

(*d*) *Poland.* Krasinski, *History of the Reformation in Poland* (2 vols., London, 1840). By the same Author,

Sketch of the Religious History of the Slavonic Nations
(Edinburgh, 1851).

(*e*) *France.* The chapters, on the Reformation, in
Michelet's General History of France, are correct and
animated. The *Student's History of France* (1 vol.,
8vo., 1862) gives a brief narrative of the Reformation
and the Civil Wars. Ranke's *History of France, especially in the 16th and 17th centuries,* is translated in part
under the title, *History of Civil Wars and Monarchy in
France, London,* 1852. The whole work, like the rest
of the series by Ranke on this era, is masterly. Among
the other valuable works on the French Reformation,
are De Felice, *History of French Protestants,* translated
·by Lobdell (1851). W. S. Browning, *History of the
Huguenots in the 16th century* (3 vols., 1829-39). [Mrs.
Marsh], *History of the Huguenots* (2 vols., 1847). Duc
D'Aumale, *Lives of the Princes of Conde* (vol. i. and ii.,
London, 1872). H. White, *The Massacre of St. Bartholomew, preceded by a narrative of the religious wars*
(London, 1868). This one of the best of the histories
of this period; it gives interesting details.

(*f*) *Netherlands.* Brandt, *History of the Reformation
in the Netherlands* (4 vols., 4to.). Engl. translation
(London, 1720). Brandt is the learned Arminian historian. His voluminous work is highly prized by scholars.
Motley, *Rise of the Dutch Republic,* 3 vols. (New York,
1856). Prescott, *History of Philip II.* (3 vols., 1855.)

(*g*) *England.* The works of the English Reformers
have been published by the Parker Society, in 54 vols.,
with a general index. The general histories of England
treat of the Reformation; as Macaulay (in his Introductory Chapter)—also, in his reviews of Ranke, and Hallam; Hume Lingard, from the Roman Catholic point
of view; Froude, etc. Hallam's *Constitutional History*

is an authority of the first rank on all legal and constitutional questions connected with the rise and progress of Protestantism in England, and is instructive on collateral points. Burnet's *History of the Reformation*, is the work of an honest writer, with extraordinary means of knowledge, but sometimes swayed by prejudice. The biographical and historical writings of Strype are of great value to the student who wishes to make a thorough study of the English Reformation. Massingberd's *History of the English Reformation* has passed through many editions. It is concise. J. H. Blunt, in his *History of the Reformation to the death of Wolsey, 1514-47* (London, 1872) represents the conservative, or High Church opinions. He bestows much praise upon Wolsey and his ideas of Reform. Neal's *History of the Puritans from the Reformation to the death of Queen Elizabeth*, is a learned account of the Reformation from the Puritan standing-point. Bacon's *Genesis of the New England Churches* is a narrative of the rise of Independency, and of the migration of the Pilgrims to Plymouth.

(*h*) *Scotland.* The *History of the Reformation*, by John Knox himself, is one of the principal sources of information. Robertson, *History of Scotland during the reigns of Mary and James VI.*, etc. McCrie's *Life of John Knox* is highly instructive. Burton, *History of Scotland to* 1688. This is the most recent, and probably the best of the histories of Scotland. It is full upon the Reformation.

(*i*) *Italy.* McCrie's *History of the Reformation in Italy*, is a standard work. M. Young's *Life of Paleario* (2 vols., 1860) throws light upon the history of Italian Protestantism.

(*j*) *Spain.* McCrie's *History of the Reformation in Spain* is the best work on the subject. Prescott's *His-*

tory of Philip II. Ticknor's *History of Spanish Litera-ture,* and Llorente's *History of the Inquisition in Spain,* may be consulted with profit.

In addition to the foregoing titles, may be mentioned Sarpi's *History of the Council of Trent,* Ranke's *History of the Popes,* Hübner's *Life of Pope Sixtus V.,* Stein-metz's *History of the Jesuits,* Isaac Taylor, *Loyola and Jesuitism iu its Rudiments.* These works bear on the rise and progress of the Catholic Reaction.

PUBLISHER'S NOTE.

A full list of "Works in general history relating to the Period of the Reformation," giving the titles in full, will be found in the *History of the Reformation* by Prof. Fisher. Those who may desire to pursue the study of this Era in any particular direction beyond the limits indicated above, will find all necessary aid in the list named.

INDEX.

247

F 5